Bastian Börsig

DISTANZ

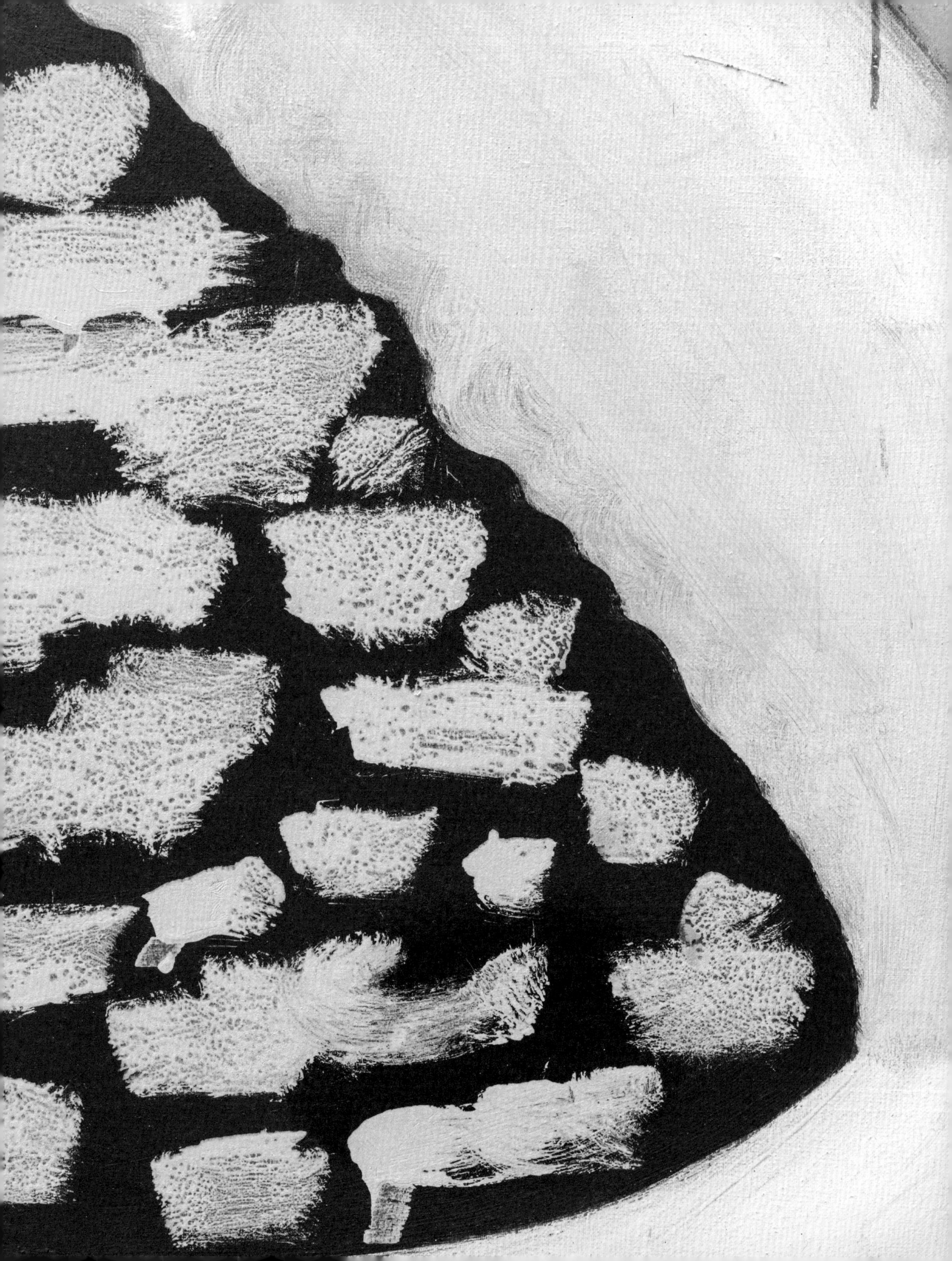

VORWORT

Alles in Bewegung irgendwie. Farbe bewegt hier Dinge und Dinge bewegen Farbe. Ohne eine bestimmte Richtung dieser Bewegung auszumachen. Bastian Börsigs Malereien scheinen einfach nie still zu stehen. Der Maler treibt in seinen großformatigen Bildern die Farben und Dinge geradezu an. Sie gestalten sich in dynamischen Veränderungsprozessen und befinden sich formal und inhaltlich stetig im Werden.

Mit diesem Prinzip extrahiert er die zufälligen und aus dem Alltag gefallenen plastischen Momente. Die augenblickliche Gegenwart plötzlicher Bilder, die keiner Zeitlichkeit folgen, Abläufe unterbrechen, Alltäglichkeiten durchkreuzen. Ungewöhnlich gewöhnlich. Sie werden fixiert und sie werden wieder verworfen. Eine räumliche Konstellation, eine seltsame Situation, die etwas in sich trägt, das genauer betrachtet werden will. Doch anstelle eines detaillierten Mikroskopierens zeigen sich diese Zustände in einer großzügigen Geste des Blow-ups. In der Vergrößerung eines Moments erscheinen Farben und Flächen, die vorher nicht da waren, tauchen Lücken auf. Sie überlagern und formieren sich zu ungegenständlichen Farbwolken, die die Leinwand verräumlichen. Zusammen mit den eigensinnigen surrealen Figurationen, die irritierend in diesen Farbräumen agieren, verdichten sie sich zu vorstellbaren Narrationen. Mit sich selbst beschäftigte Formationen, die sich an Gegenständen reiben und dadurch herrlich absurde Züge annehmen. Abstraktion der Alltäglichkeit. Etwas erinnert an etwas, was es nicht ist. Und dennoch glaubt man es zu erkennen.

Darüber denke ich nach, wenn ich diese Malereien betrachte. Vage möchte ich benennen, was ich hier sehe. Die banalen und eigenartigen Dinge, die sich immer wieder in etwas Anderes verwandeln, Handlungen ausführen und vorführen. Requisiten und Protagonisten in gleicher Weise. Sie werden zum Dreh- und Angelpunkt der Bilder, durch die mir der Maler vermeintlich Geschichten offenbart, die ich mir als Betrachterin aber tatsächlich selber ausdenke.

Farben, aufgespießt auf Tischbeinen. Farben, die sich kurz ausruhen, aber eigentlich schon wieder auf dem Sprung sind. Ein Kamm, der versucht, eine Fläche zu zähmen. Alltagsgegenstände, vor allem Behälter und Möbel. Große Dinge, aber eben auch der Kamm, der ist klein. Wie die Schühchen. Es gibt Tassen, die Beine haben, stehen und sich drehen. Tiere und Bäume, die sich biegen, weich wie Gummi. Eine Weltkugel auf drei Beinen. Sie läuft davon. Eine Kartoffel, die zwischen zwei Pfeilern hängt. Etwas, das in einer Kiste sitzt, und einer mit Konservendose, vielleicht ein Schaf, das schläft, Stöcke in einer Box, Sessel und Gewitterwolke, holzbeinige Zahnlücken und Querköpfe. Diese Gestalten sind da, gegenwärtig. Was für ein Einblick wird mir hier offenbart? Was offenbare ich mir selber, wenn ich durch dieses Fenster der Absurdität blicke? Das Grinsen steht mir dabei ebenso gut wie diesen Bildern. Ich fühle mich ertappt, die ganz normale unbeholfene Alltäglichkeit in diesem Wahnwitz zu entdecken.

Isabella Gerstner, 2016

UNTITLED [2016, Detail]
Oil, lacquer, charcoal on canvas | 280 × 200 cm

PREFACE

Everything is somehow in motion. Color sets things in motion, and things stir up the colors. Their agitation does not add up to movement in any definite direction: Bastian Börsig's paintings just seem to be never at rest. Creating his large canvases, he positively urges his colors and things into action. They take shape in dynamic processes of transmutation, and their substance as much as their form is always becoming.

This creative principle lets him isolate serendipitous moments of sculptural clarity in which the everyday falls away. The momentary presence of sudden sights subject to no temporal order, images that disrupt processes and defeat the trivial. Extraordinarily ordinary. He captures their likeness and then discards them. A constellation in space, a peculiar situation pregnant with something that warrants closer examination. Yet instead of a microscopic gaze on the detail, he presents these states of affairs by blowing them up to generously dimensioned paintings. The enlarged vision of the instant reveals colors and surfaces that did not exist before; blanks emerge, overlap, coalesce into nonrepresentational clouds of color that endow the canvas with spatial depth. Together with the idiosyncratic surreal figurations whose irritating operations unfold in these chromatic spaces, they limn dense if forever imaginary narratives. Self-involved formations that, in chafing at objectivity, take on an air of magnificent absurdity. The abstraction of the everyday; objects reminiscent of what they are not: and yet we seem to recognize them.

That is what I contemplate as I look at these paintings. I feel a vague desire to put a name on what I see. These banal and odd things in perpetual transformation into something else, performing and demonstrating actions. Props and protagonists at once. They become the pivots of these pictures in which the painter appears to divulge stories to me, though in reality it is I, the beholder, who concocts them.

Colors speared on the legs of a table. Colors catching their breath but already in a rush to be elsewhere. A comb trying to tame a surface. Mundane objects, primarily containers and furniture. Big boxy things, but then here is the comb, so small. Like the little shoes. There are cups that have legs, standing and gyrating. Animals and trees, soft as rubber, bending themselves into shapes. A globe on three legs running away. A potato suspended between two pillars. Something sitting in a crate, someone holding a can, what may be a sleeping sheep, sticks in a box, armchair and thunderhead, peg-legged tooth gaps and oddballs. These figures are there, are here and now. What sorts of glimpses behind the curtain are being vouchsafed to me? What do I reveal to myself peering through this window of absurdity? The grin on my face suits me no less than these pictures. I feel like I have been caught in the act: I have discovered the perfectly normal awkward ordinariness in the absurd.

Isabella Gerstner, 2016

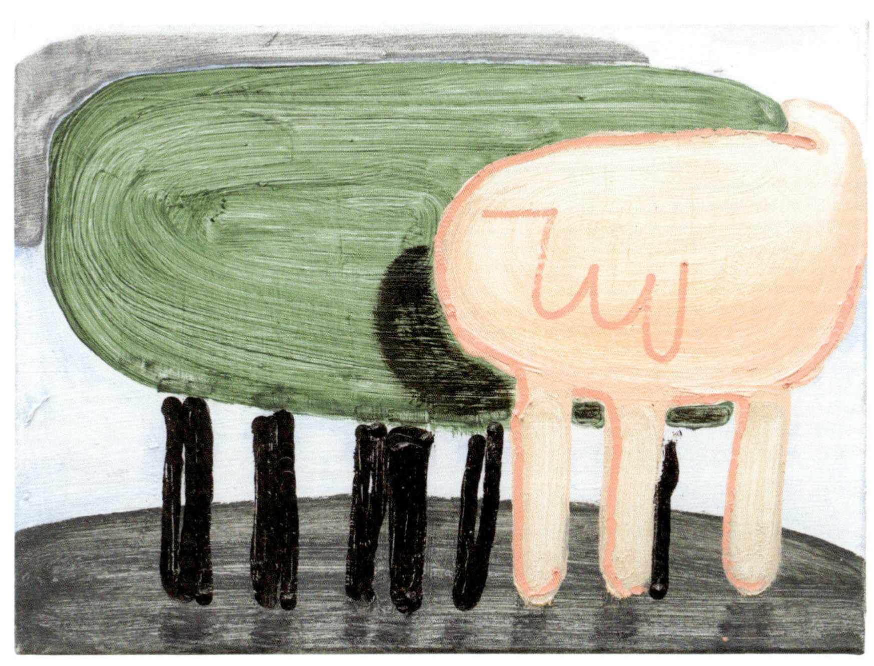

UNTITLED [2014]
Oil on canvas | 42 × 56 cm

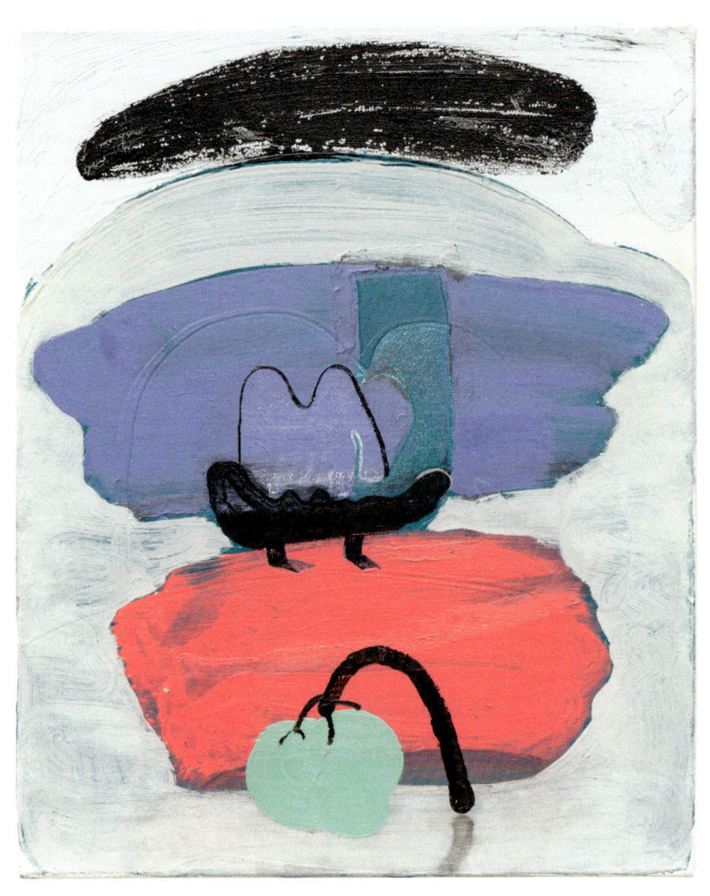

UNTITLED [2014]
Oil, lacquer on canvas | 50 × 40 cm

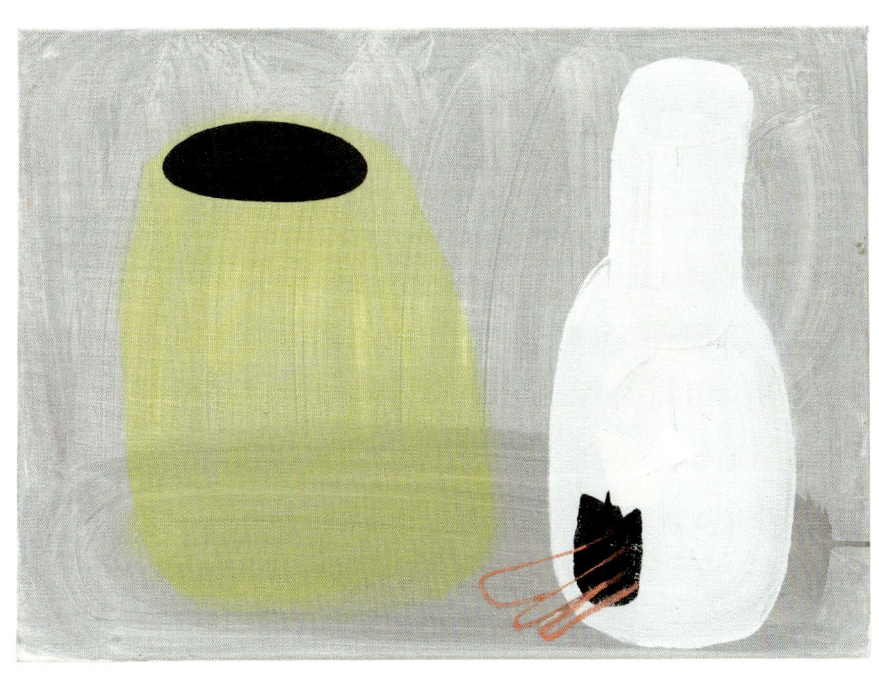

UNTITLED [2014]
Oil, lacquer on canvas | 45 × 60 cm

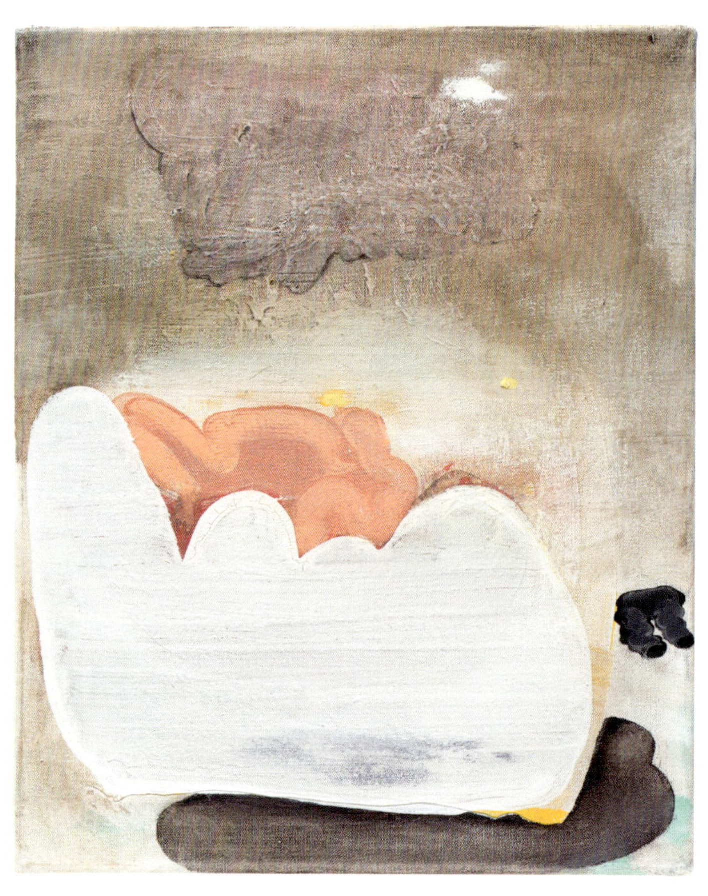

UNTITLED [2014]
Oil, lacquer on canvas | 50 × 40 cm

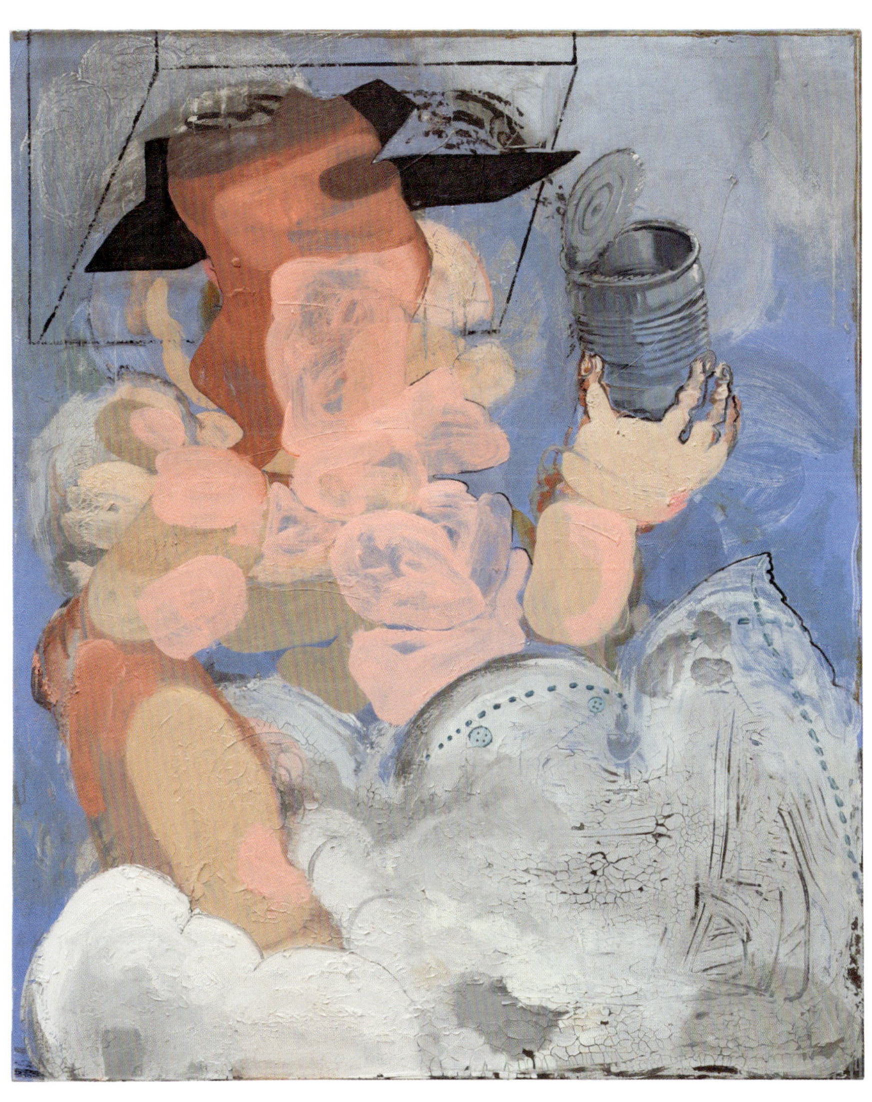

UNTITLED [2014]
Oil, lacquer on canvas | 155 × 125 cm

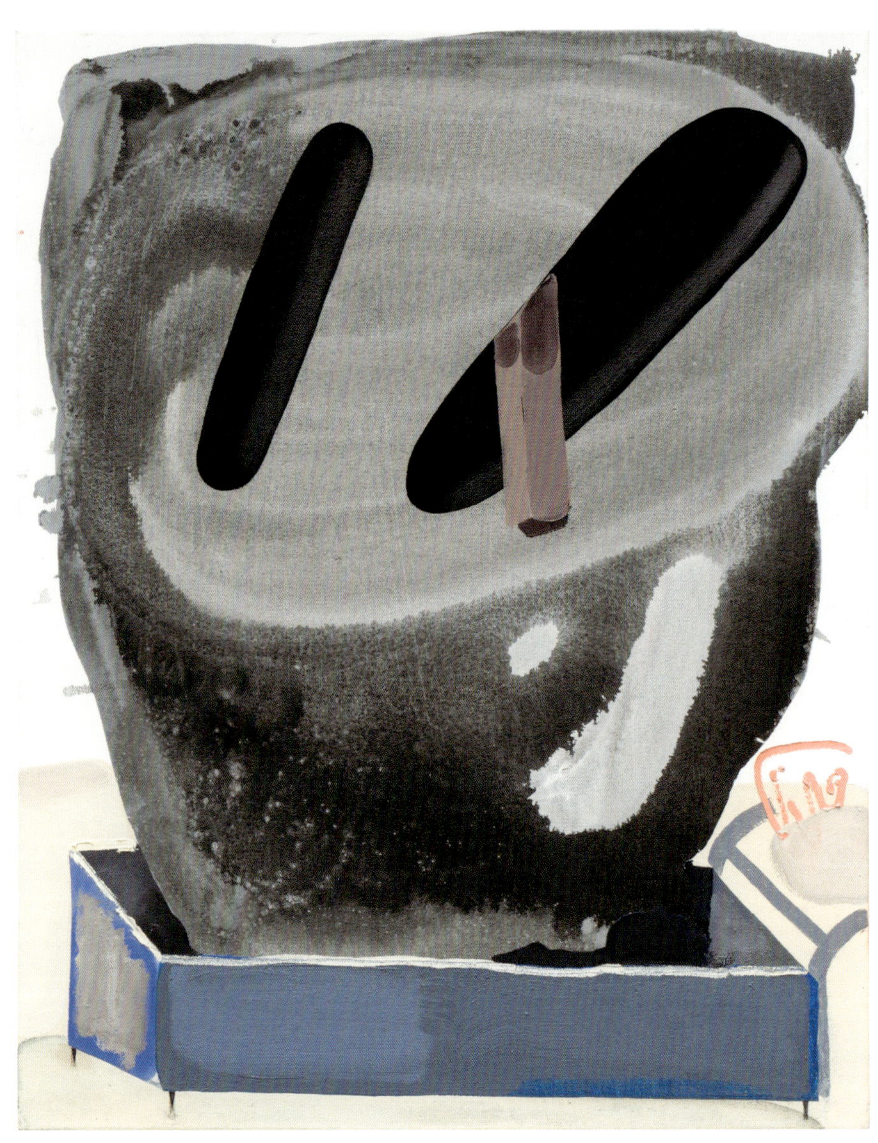

UNTITLED [2015]
Oil, lacquer on canvas | 90 × 70 cm

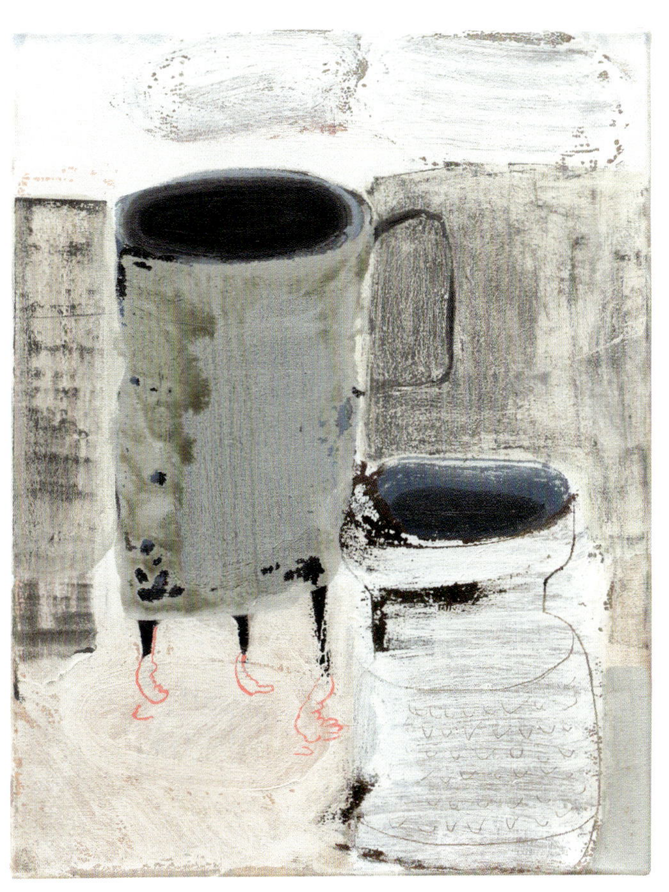

UNTITLED [2014]
Oil, lacquer on canvas | 60 × 45 cm

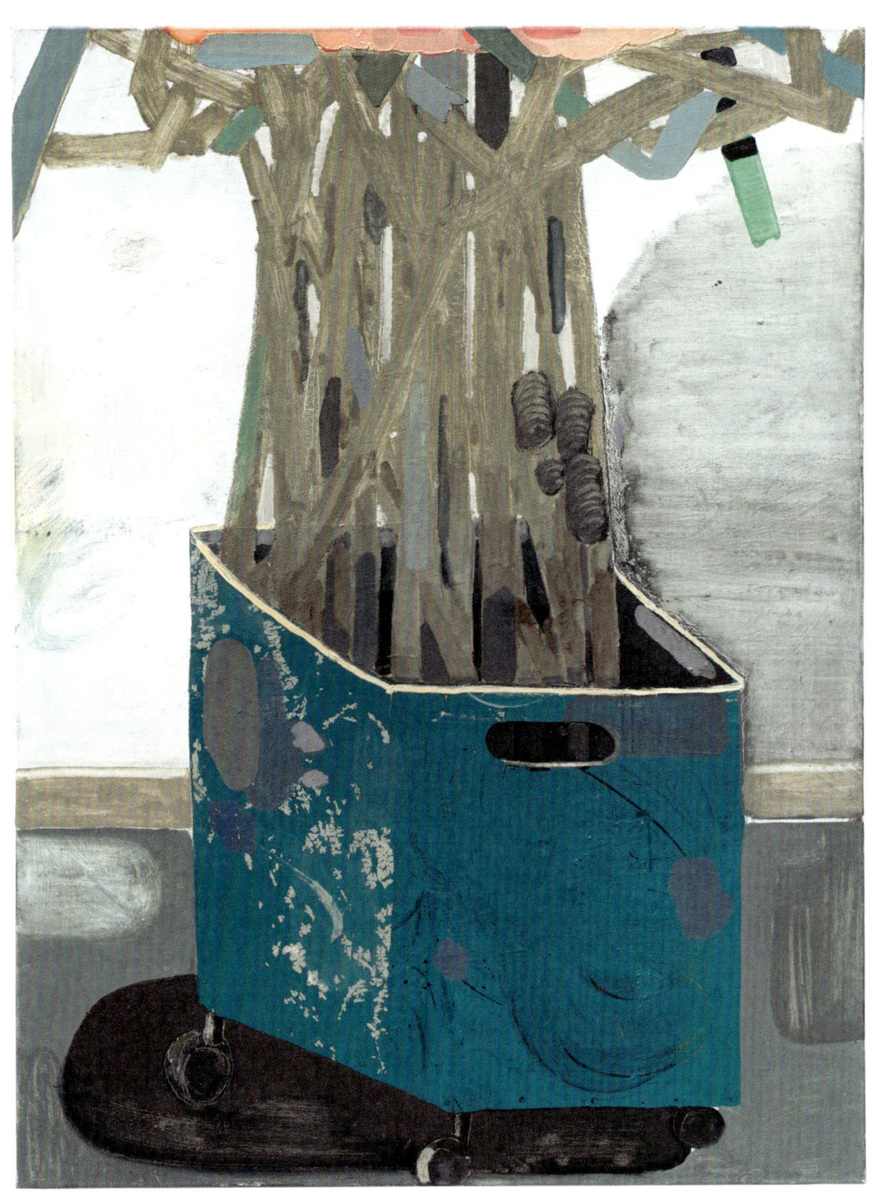

UNTITLED [2014]
Oil, lacquer on canvas | 160 × 120 cm

„ICH SEHE BILDER UND MACHE BILDER!“*– BASTIAN BÖRSIGS MALEREI

Die Frage nach der mimetischen Funktion der Malerei zu stellen, also das Medium anhand seiner Abbildhaftigkeit zu untersuchen, mag nach über 100 Jahren moderner Bildverwerfungen ermüdend klingen. Im Fall von Bastian Börsig erscheint dies auf den ersten Blick geradezu als Negativfolie. Doch seine Bilder fallen nicht vom Himmel. Ihre Genese ist eingespannt in einen verschlungenen Prozess, an dessen Anfang die Wirklichkeit steht bzw. der sinnliche Abglanz der Wirklichkeit im Körper des Künstlers.

Börsig spricht von „Auslösern“ eines Bildes und meint damit visuelle oder auch emotionale Eindrücke, die sich aus seiner Wahrnehmung der Realität speisen. Man erfährt etwas über den Verwandlungsvorgang der Wirklichkeit – über die Migration der Bilder – anhand der spärlichen, restfigurativen Elemente in seinen Werken, die Börsig den Betrachtern als ersten Blickanker darbietet. So erkennt man in den durchgängig unbetitelten Leinwänden unter anderem ein Sofa, einen Eimer, eine Kiste, eine Kommode mit Tellern oder einen roten Tisch mit Schublade. Aber die zeichenhaft abstrahierten Dinge ergeben rein sachlich überhaupt keinen Sinn, abgesehen von den Umrissen eines nach perspektivischen Grundsätzen erfahrenen Raumes, zu dem etwa ein Verhältnis von oben und unten, die Existenz von Licht und Schatten oder auch angedeutete Fluchtungen zählen. Es ist die Ahnung eines Körpers, wie man ihn unter Umständen mit geschlossenen Augen „sehen“ würde. Diese Spuren der Wirklichkeitswahrnehmung sind größtenteils häuslichen Ursprungs, mit Verweisen auf Einrichtungsgegenstände oder Küchenutensilien, und in ihrer Banalität auf der untersten Ebene der Bildstruktur begreift man sofort, dass sie hier gar nicht das tragende Thema sind.

Gemäß einer in der Philosophie des späten 17. und frühen 18. Jahrhunderts entwickelten Begrifflichkeit können wir nicht die Dinge an sich, sondern nur ihr von unserer Wahrnehmung übermitteltes Abbild erkennen. Die Realität ist ein Schein unseres Bewusstseins. Das ist die perzeptive Umkehrung von Platons Ideenlehre, der anhand seines Höhlengleichnisses beschrieb, wie sich die Wirklichkeit dem menschlichen Bewusstsein als Schattenspiel von eigentlichen, nicht direkt erfahrbaren Entitäten darbietet. Während Platons Ideen völlig unabhängig vom Menschen existieren, richtet der von John Locke und George Berkeley ausgebildete Sensualismus sein Augenmerk auf die Kontamination der Wirklichkeit durch den menschlichen Geist als wichtigste Instanz. An diesem historischen Moment sind die Ursprünge eines

* aus einem vom Künstler 2014 verfassten Selbstzeugnis

neuen Bildbegriffs nachweisbar, der in das Paradigma der Moderne eingeschrieben wurde. Nicht mehr die äußere Realität ist wesentlich, sondern eine innere Wirklichkeit, die nun das Verhältnis von Künstler und Werk entscheidend prägt.

Das Gesehene, Erfahrene, Erinnerte ist bei Bastian Börsig das lose Gerüst für eine umfassende Verstellung, die sich erst im Prozess des Malens manifestiert. Dieser Vorgang ist weitgehend offen und dialogisch angelegt im Verhältnis des Künstlers zur Oberfläche des Bildes. Dabei bedient er sich eines vielfältigen technischen Repertoires, zu dem unter anderem die Kontraste von pastosen, dickfarbig behandelten Partien und dünnflüssig aufgetragenen Flächen gehören, in denen Pinselspuren sowie Trocknungsnasen als Spuren des Gemachtseins hervortreten. Die starke Materialität des Farbauftrags, der mitunter auch verrieben oder eingekratzt wird, bannt Börsig durch scharf gesetzte Objektkanten oder mitunter comicartige Lineaturen, die zu der Aura von Beschwingtheit und der grundsätzlichen Positivität seiner Bilder beitragen. Er kombiniert Ölfarbe gerne mit Kohle oder Lack, was im letzteren Fall zum eigentümlichen Abblättern oder Reißen der Farbschicht führt, wenn sie mit langsamer trocknenden Schichten aus Öl unterlegt ist. Das dosiert eingesetzte Stilmittel des Krakelees vermittelt den Anschein einer Abnutzung oder auch altersbedingten Beschädigung der Maloberfläche und kontrastiert wirksam mit dem vorherrschenden Vokabular der Bilder von weichen, oftmals in Pastelltönen gehaltenen Formen.

Das kann man virtuos nennen, wie Börsig die in den unterschiedlichen Techniken aufgehobenen Kräfte freisetzt und in eine fragile Balance bringt, in der sich Motiv- und Malschichten spannungsvoll verschränken und teilweise überlagern. Sie verschleiern und filtern den ursprünglichen Bildimpuls und verleihen dem Werk ein vom Körper des Künstlers unabhängiges Eigenleben. Dahinter steht keine surrealistische Technik, die dem Unterbewusstsein und dem Zufall die Bildhoheit überlässt. Dafür sind die bildimmanenten Operationen zu kalkuliert auf eine wirkungsvolle Komposition ausgerichtet. Zu spüren ist jedoch ein grundsätzlich spekulatives Verhältnis zur Realität und zwar in dem Sinne, dass Börsigs Malerei Strukturen der Dinge aufdeckt, die mit der herkömmlichen begrifflichen Erfassung der Welt keine Beziehung mehr haben.

Marc Wellmann 2016

“I SEE PICTURES AND I MAKE PICTURES!”*— THE PAINTINGS OF BASTIAN BÖRSIG

After more than a century of modernist eruptions have broken up the painting’s surface, it may seem tiresome to raise the question of its mimetic function—to scrutinize the medium with a view to its representational quality. At first glance, Bastian Börsig’s work would appear to discourage and indeed positively deny such an inquiry. Yet his pictures do not come out of nowhere. Their genesis is intertwined with a complex process that originates in reality, or its sensory reflection in the artist’s body.

Börsig speaks of “triggers” that prompt a picture: visual, or sometimes emotional, impressions that derive from his perception of reality. We can learn something about the transmutation of reality—the migration of pictures—by examining the vestigial figurative elements he offers to the beholder’s gaze as an initial anchor. On his canvases, which are always untitled, we can variously espy a sofa, a bucket, a box, a dresser with plates, or a red table with a drawer. But these objects, whittled down by abstraction to mere symbols, do not make any sense when read purely as what they are; all they do is limn the basic features of a space conceived in keeping with the principles of perspective, such as the relation between above and below, the existence of light and shadow, or intimations of alignment and depth. It is the apprehension of a solid object, comparable to what, in certain circumstances, one might “see” with closed eyes. These traces of perceived reality are largely domestic in origin, references to furniture or kitchen utensils, and their banal presence on the lowest level of the pictorial structure readily indicates that they are not its true purport.

According to a conceptual scheme developed by philosophers in the late seventeenth and early eighteenth centuries, we are incapable of cognition of things as they are in themselves; we only grasp their images as transmitted by our perceptual organs. Reality is a semblance created by our consciousness. That is the empiricist inversion of Plato’s theory of forms; his allegory of the cave described how reality presented itself to human consciousness as a shadow theater of truly substantive entities that eluded direct cognition. Plato’s ideas have absolute existence independent of man. John Locke’s and George Berkeley’s sensualism, by contrast, focuses on how the human mind, as the central agent of knowledge, contaminates reality. It marks the historic moment to which we can trace the emergence of a new conception of the picture, one that subsequently informed the modernist paradigm. It is not

*from a statement by the artist [2014]

outward reality that matters; instead, an inner reality now crucially defines the relationship between the artist and his work.

What he sees, experiences, remembers serves Bastian Börsig as the loose scaffold for an encompassing dissimulation that only gradually manifests itself as he paints. His creative process is as open as possible and structured as a dialogue in which the artist's relation to the painting's surface unfolds. Börsig commands a wide repertoire of techniques, including the deft use of contrasts between areas covered with pastose layers of thick paint and others treated with diluted paint; traces of brushwork and paint runs and drips bear witness to the work's facture. The powerful physical presence of the paint layers — the artist sometimes also rubs them on or scratches drying layers — is held at bay by sharply delineated edges of objects or ensembles of contours that sometimes recall cartoons, adding to the aura of lively good cheer his pictures exude. He likes to combine oil paint with charcoal or lacquers; a coat of the latter over layers of oil paint that dries more slowly produces a distinctive peeling or cracking of the surface. Used in moderation, such craquelure is a stylistic device that creates a semblance of abrasion or aging, in an effective contrast with the prevailing pictorial vocabulary of soft shapes often painted in pastel hues.

Unleashing the forces implicit in his various techniques and bringing them into a delicate balance in which divergent motivic strata and multiple coats of paint are interwoven and sometimes overlap to great effect, Börsig brings a virtuoso's touch to his craft. His layers veil and filter the initial pictorial impulse, endowing the work with a life independent of the artist's body. His is not a Surrealist technique that cedes authority over the painting to the subconscious and to chance: the operations immanent to the composition are too carefully calculated for maximum impact. Still, one senses a fundamentally speculative approach to reality, in the sense that Börsig's painting unearths structures of things that have broken free of the conventional conceptual framework in which we apprehend our world.

Marc Wellmann 2016

UNTITLED [2012]
Oil, lacquer on canvas | 295 × 210 cm

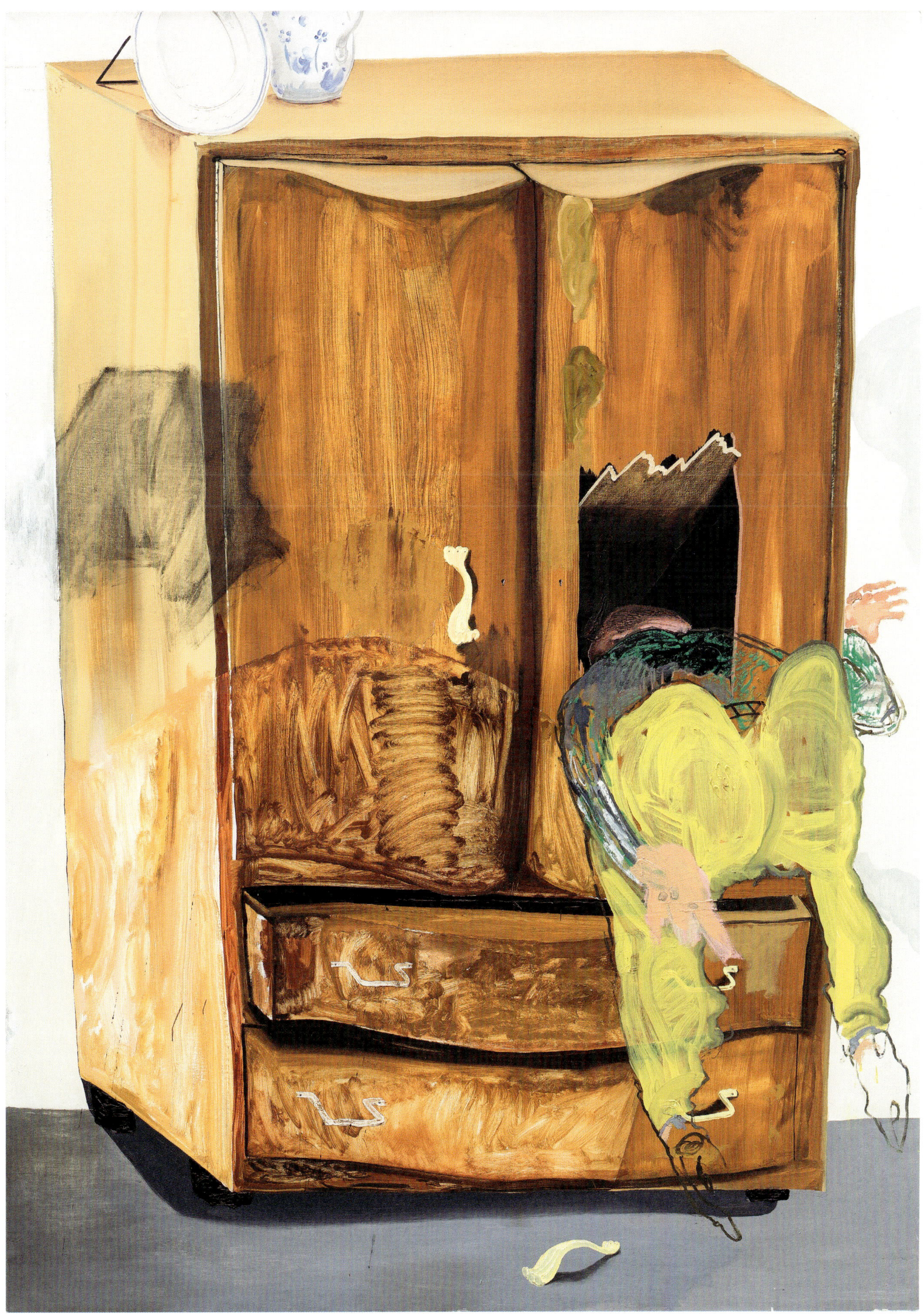

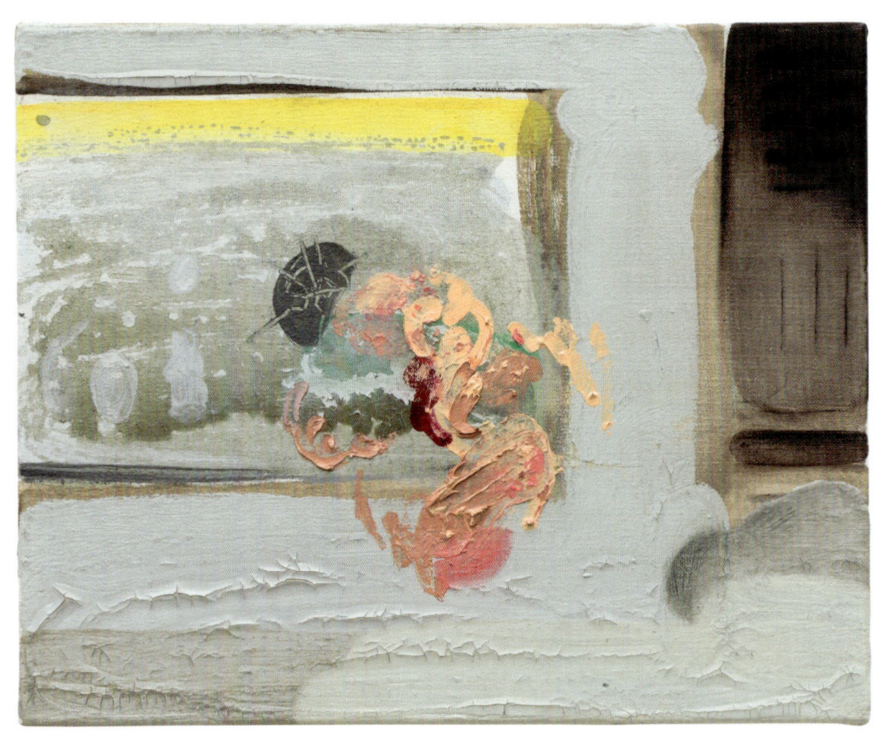

UNTITLED [2013]
Oil, lacquer on canvas | 34 × 41 cm

UNTITLED [2013]
Oil, lacquer on canvas | 285 × 200 cm

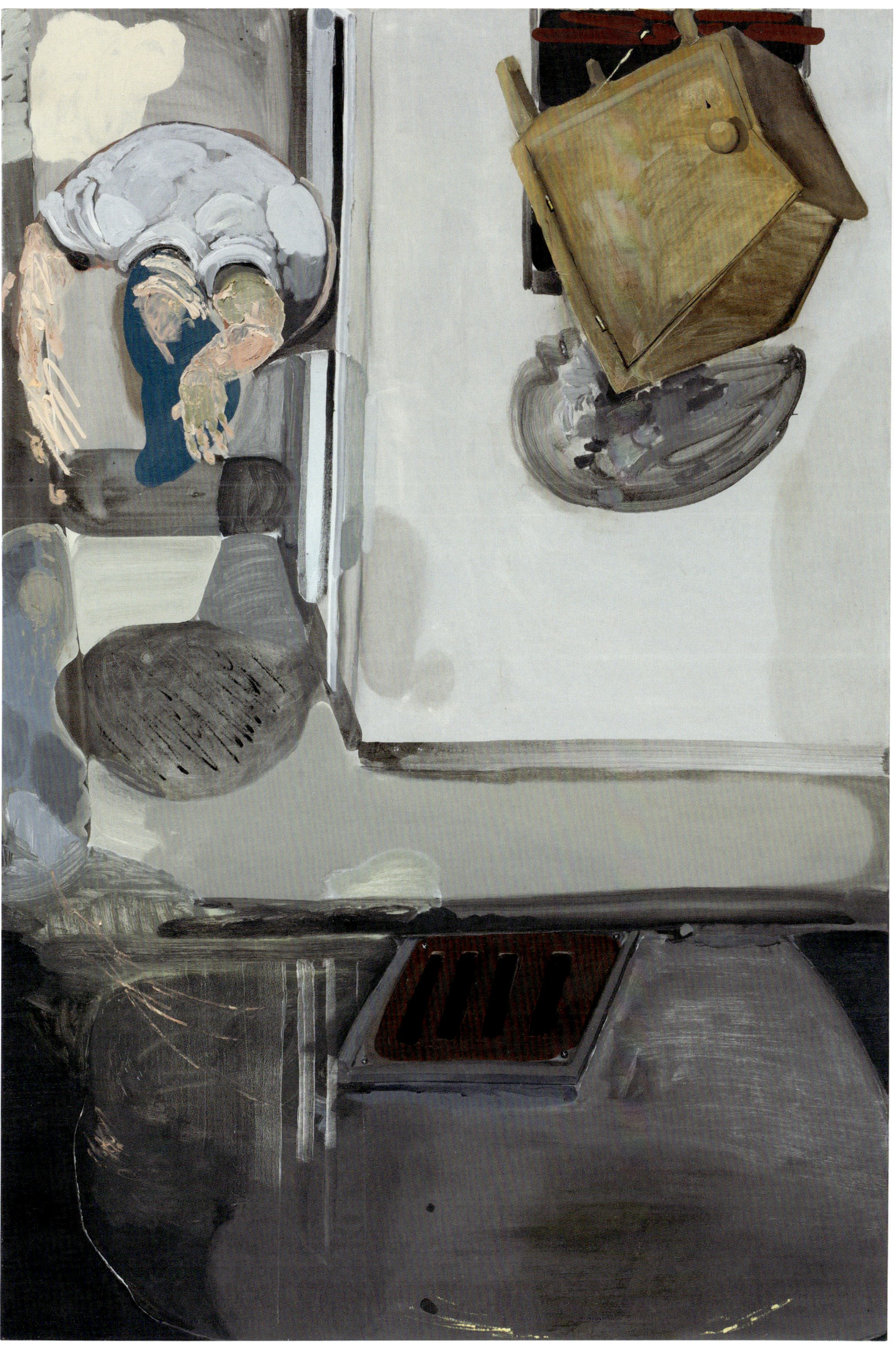

UNTITLED [2016]
Oil, lacquer, charcoal on canvas | 280 × 200 cm

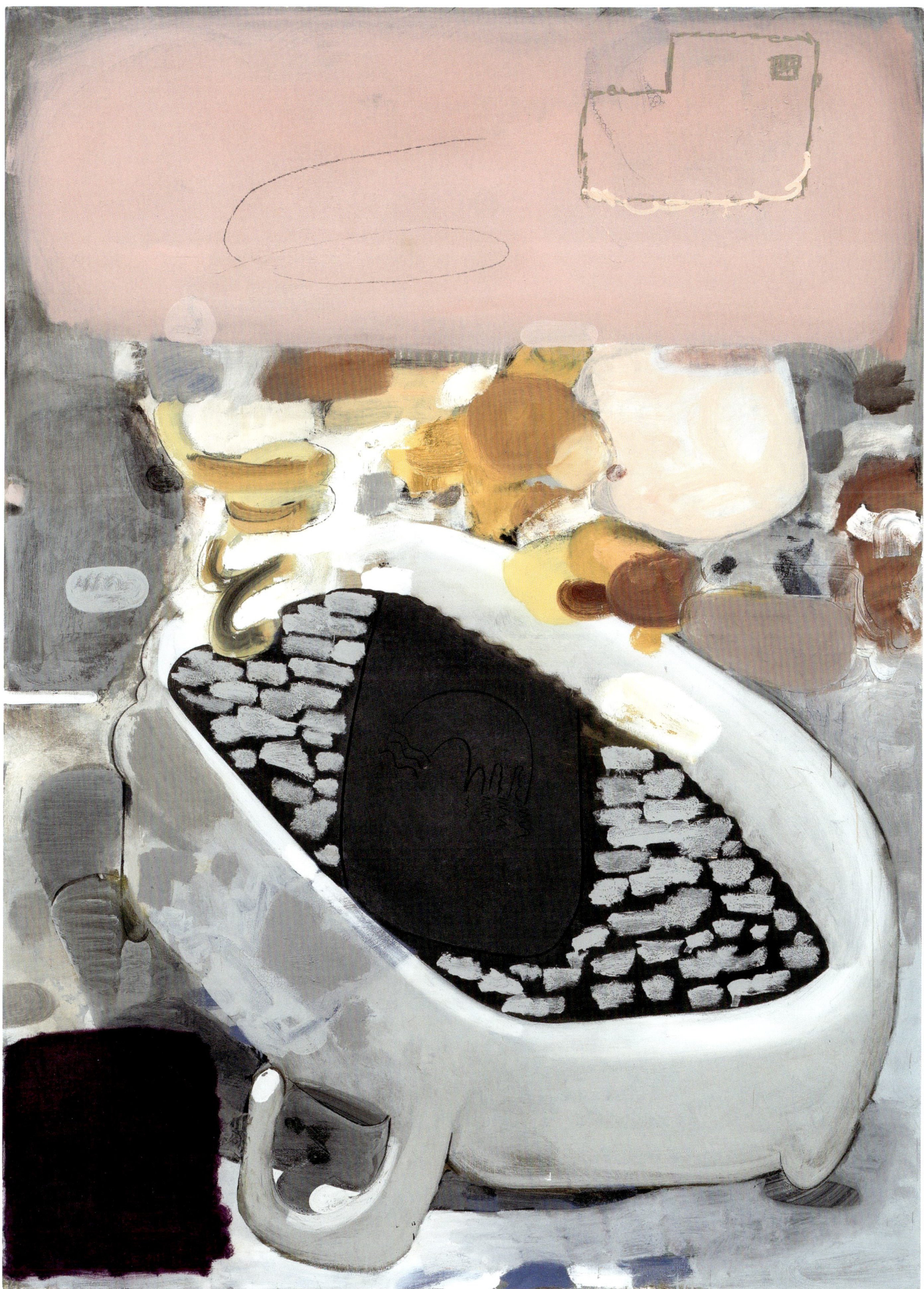

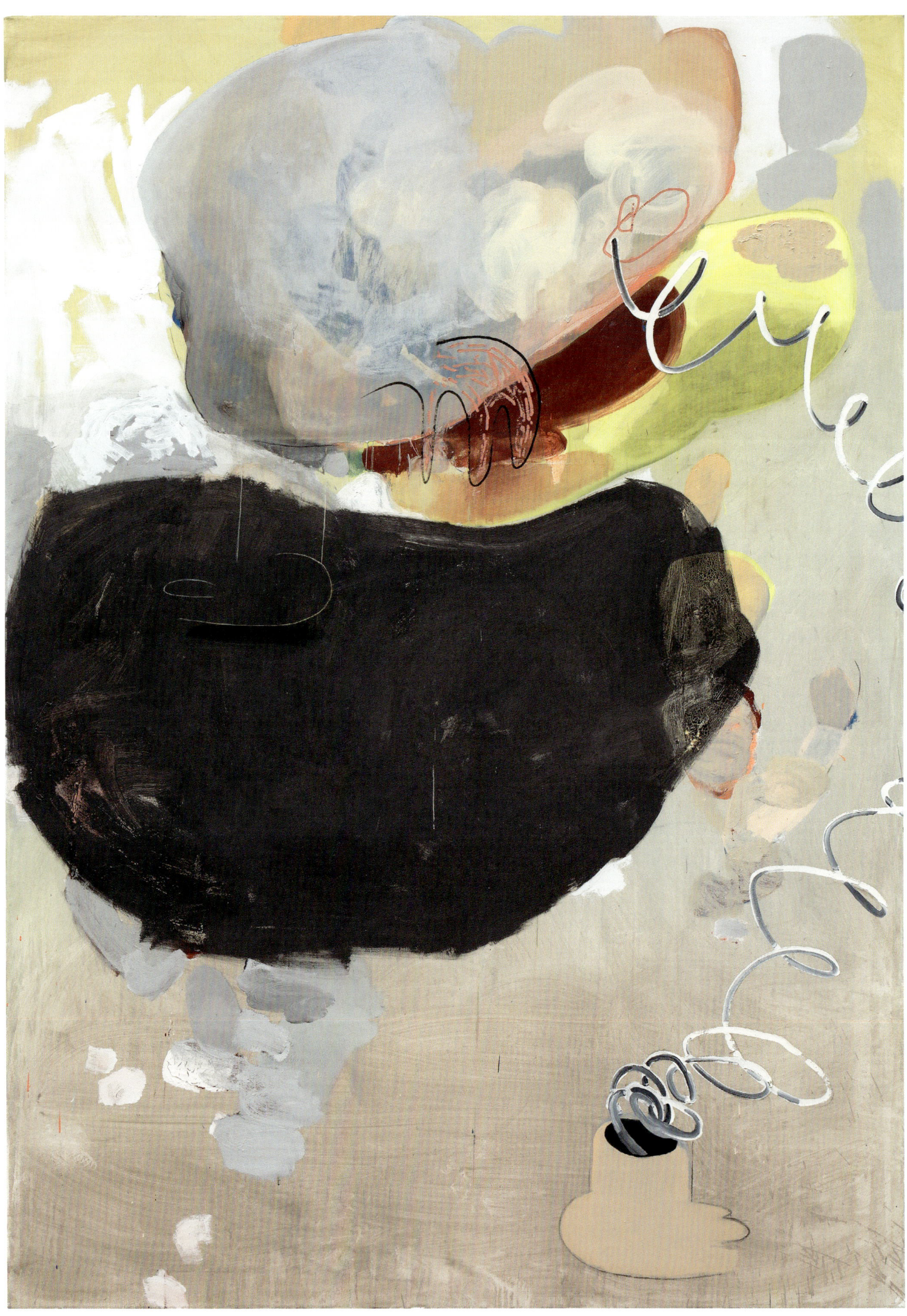

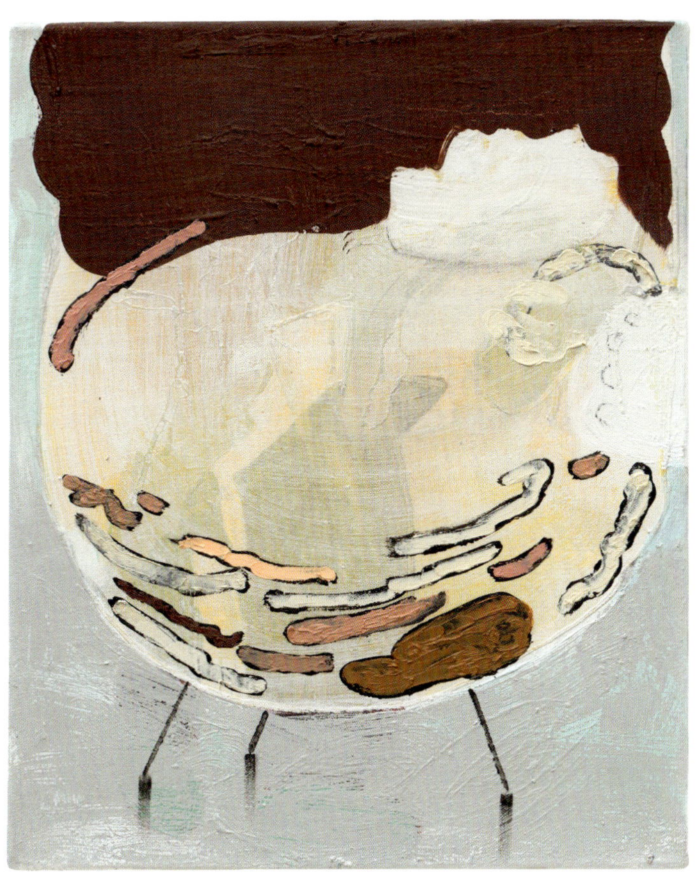

UNTITLED [2014]
Oil, lacquer on canvas | 280 × 200 cm

UNTITLED [2014]
Oil, lacquer on canvas | 50 × 40 cm

UNTITLED [2016]

Oil, lacquer, charcoal on canvas | 200 × 170 cm

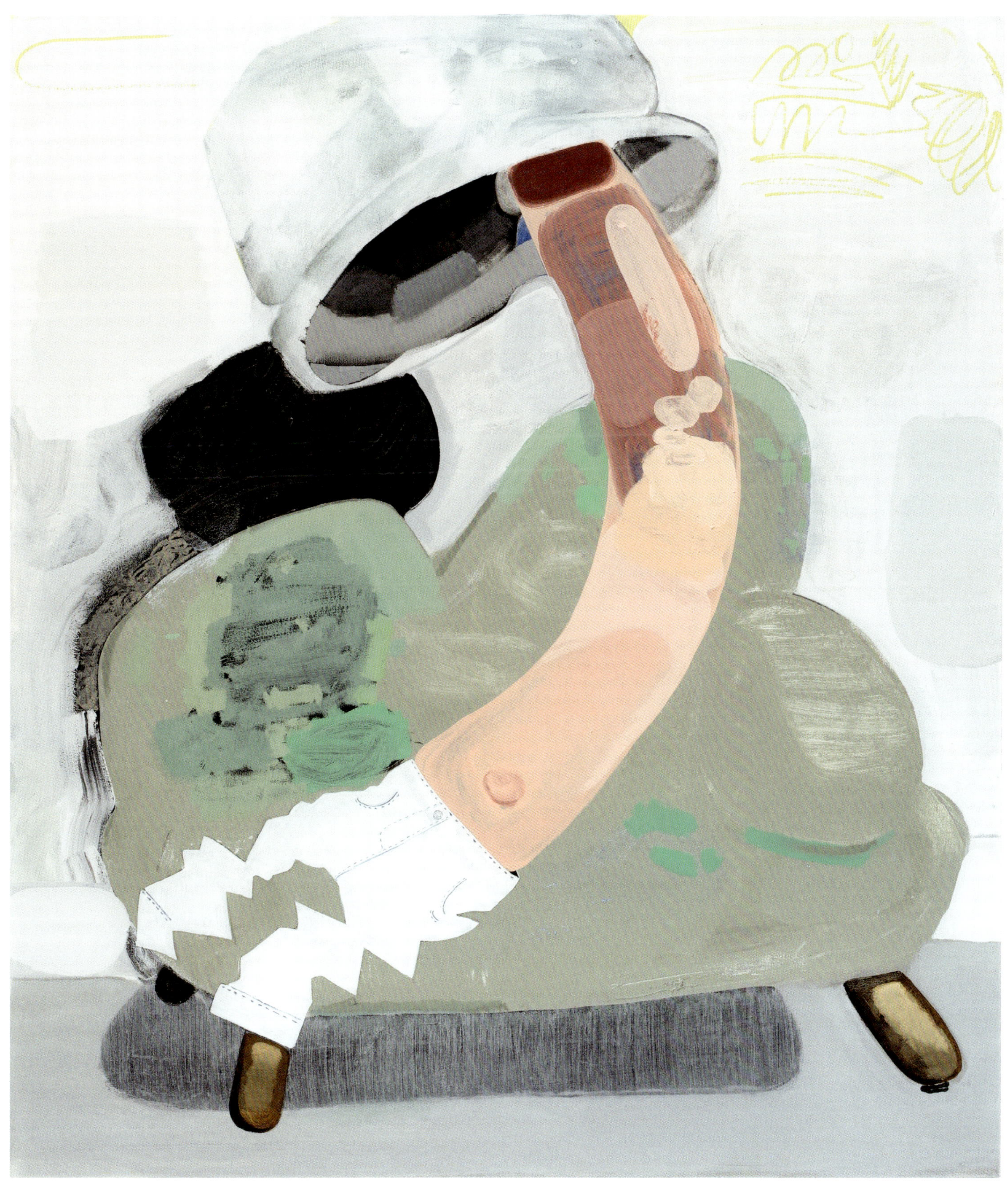

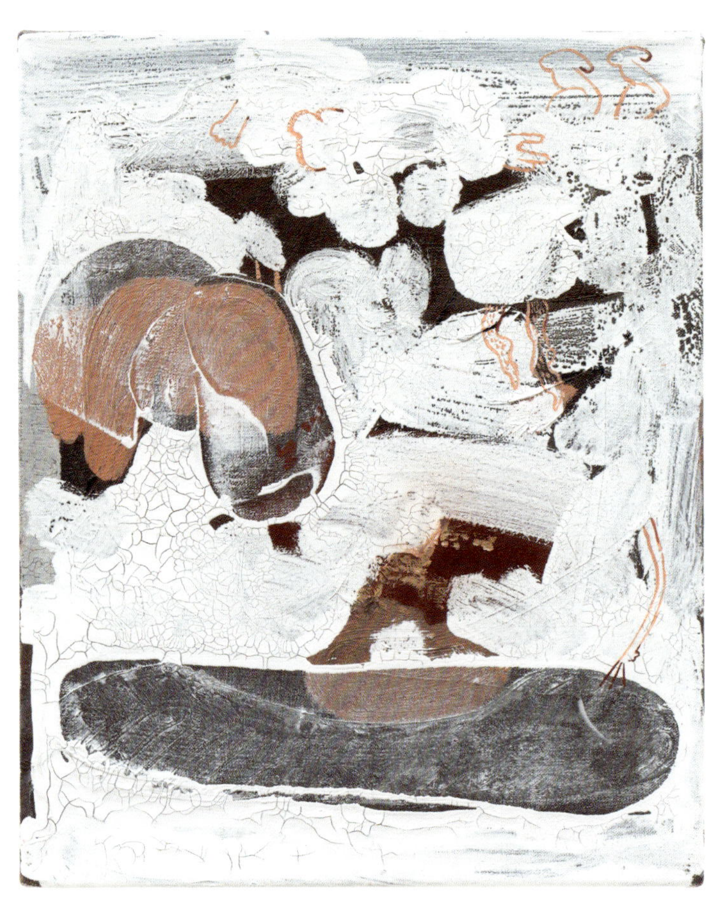

UNTITLED [2014]
Oil, lacquer on canvas | 50 × 40 cm

UNTITLED [2015]
Oil, lacquer on canvas | 297 × 213 cm

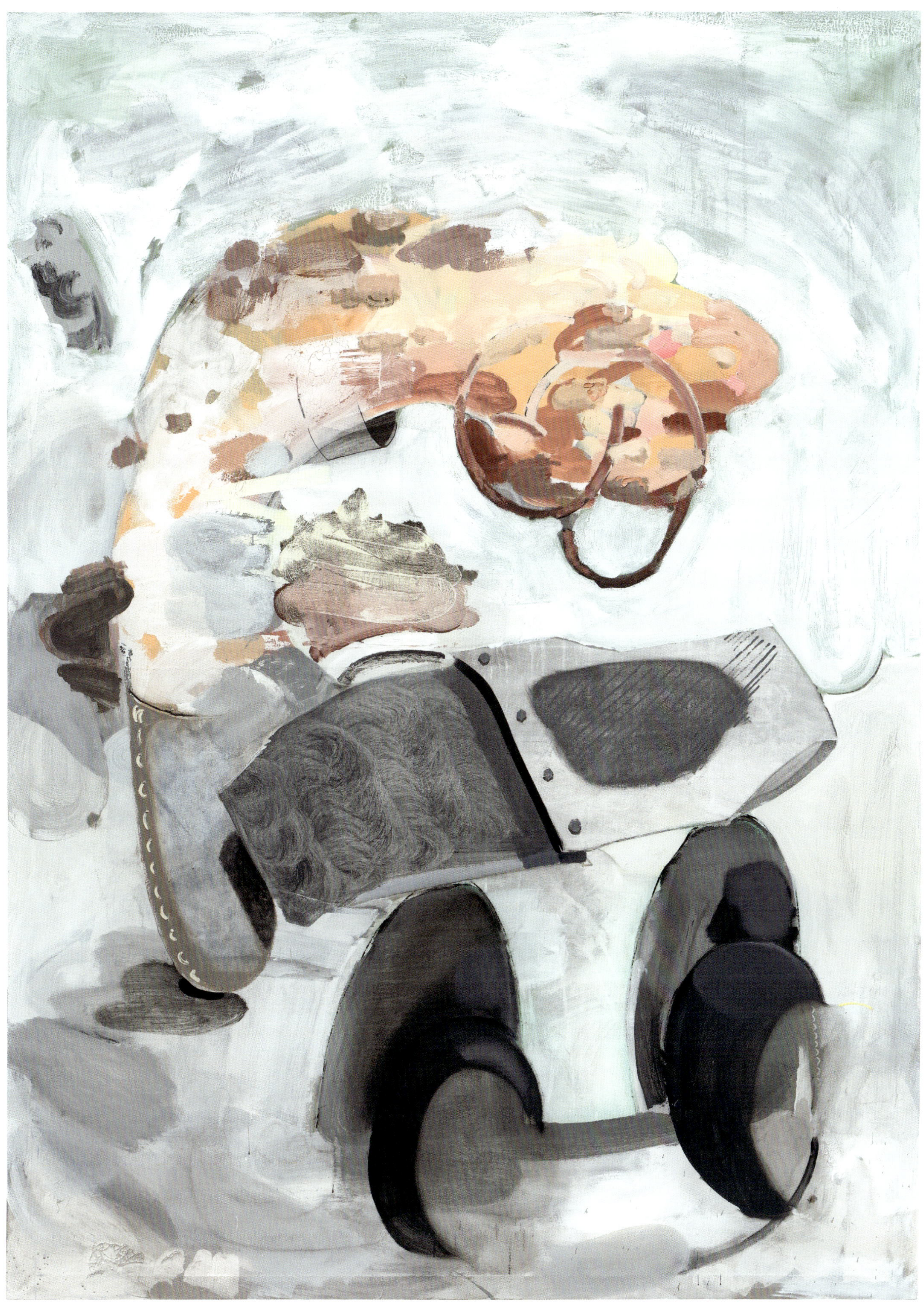

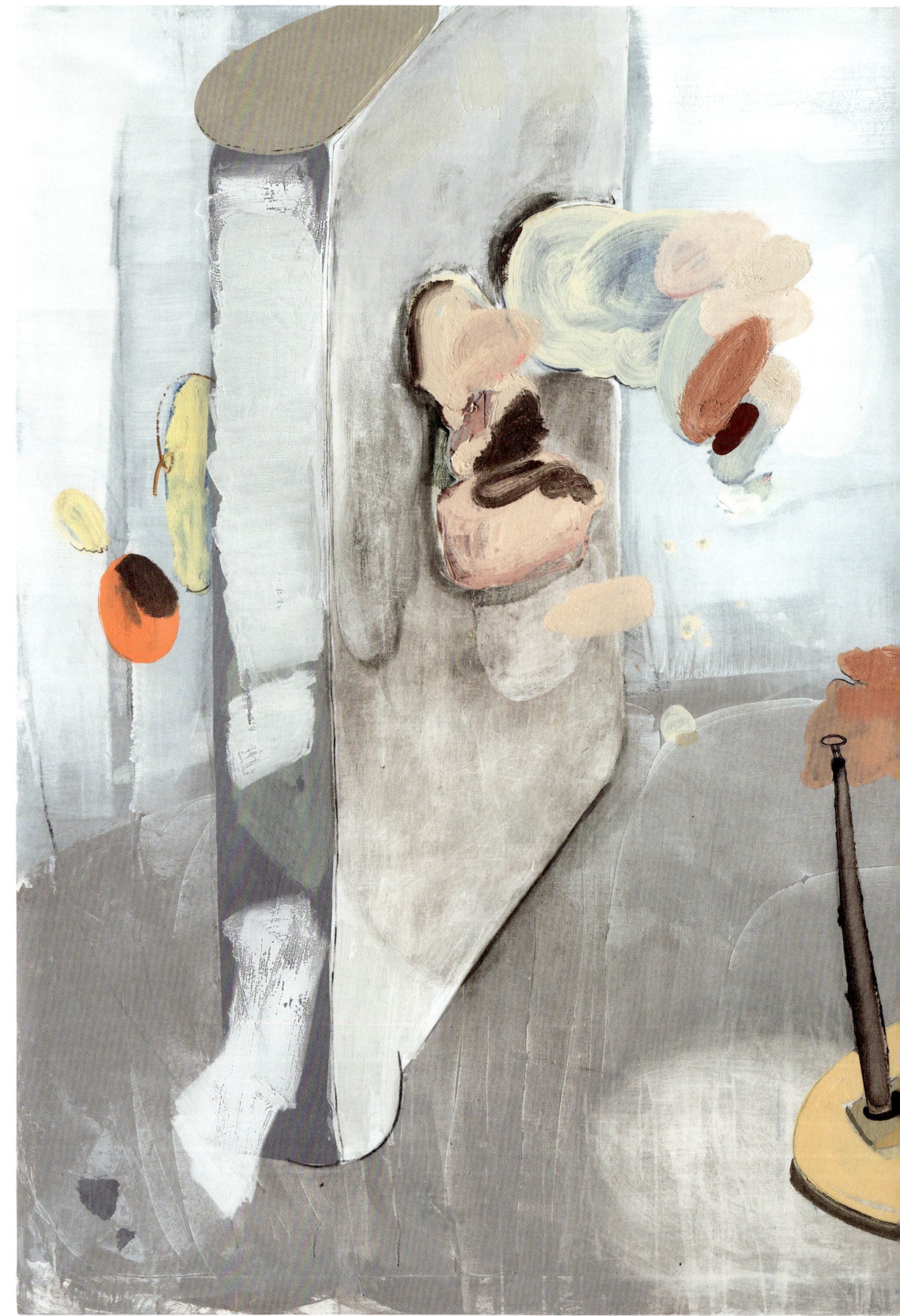

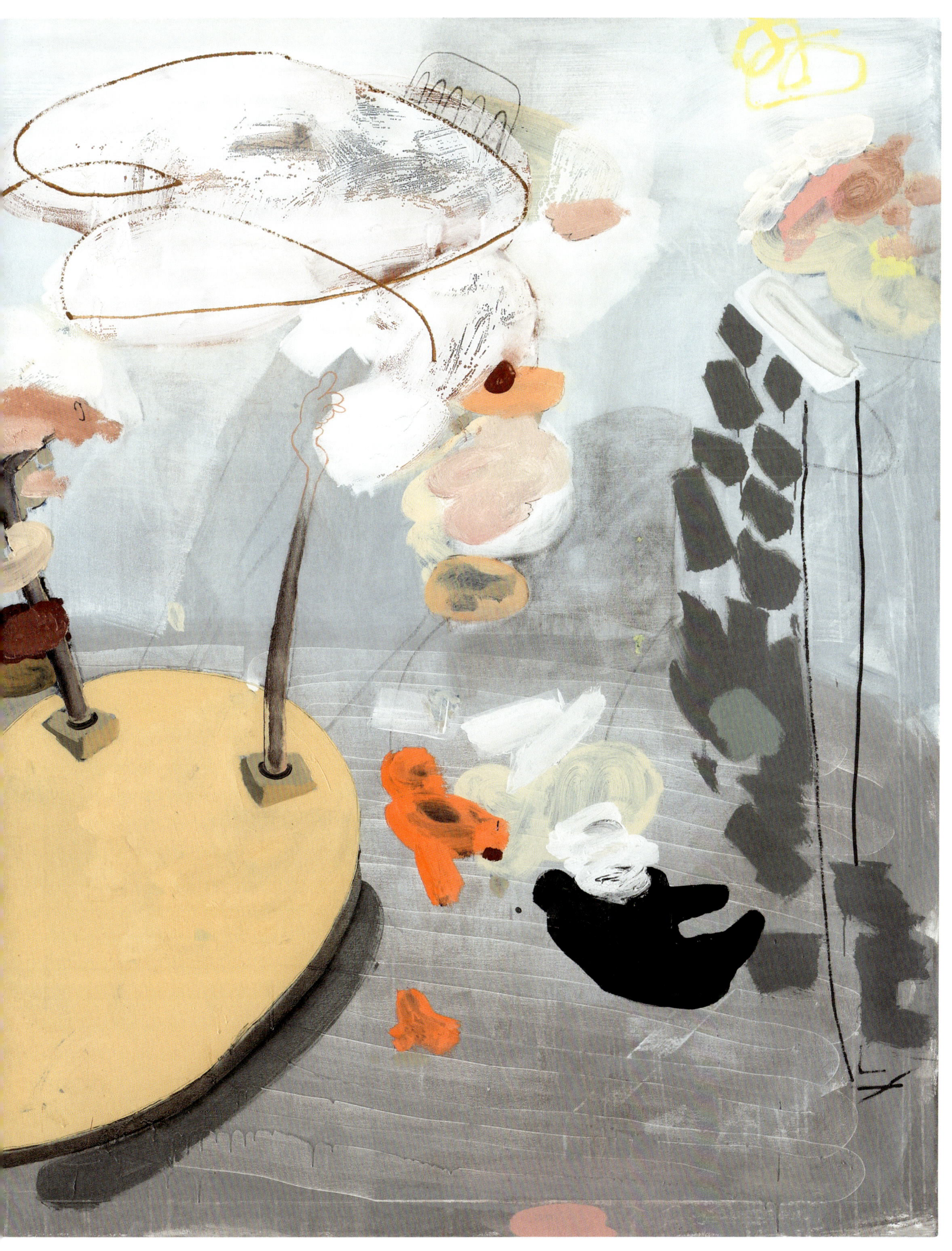

UNTITLED [2015]
Oil, lacquer, charcoal on canvas | 200 × 295 cm

UNTITLED [2014]
Oil, lacquer on canvas | 285 × 200 cm

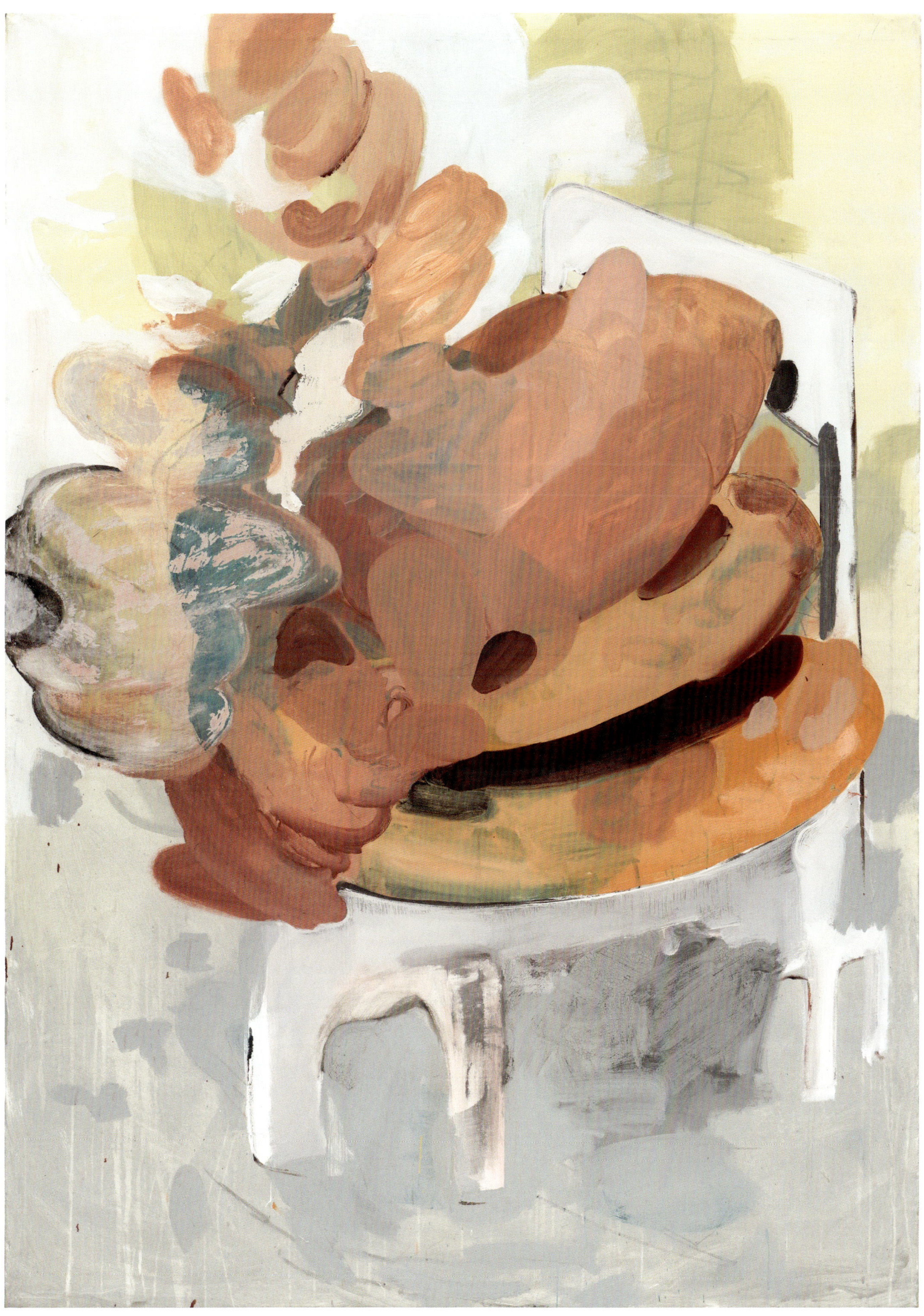

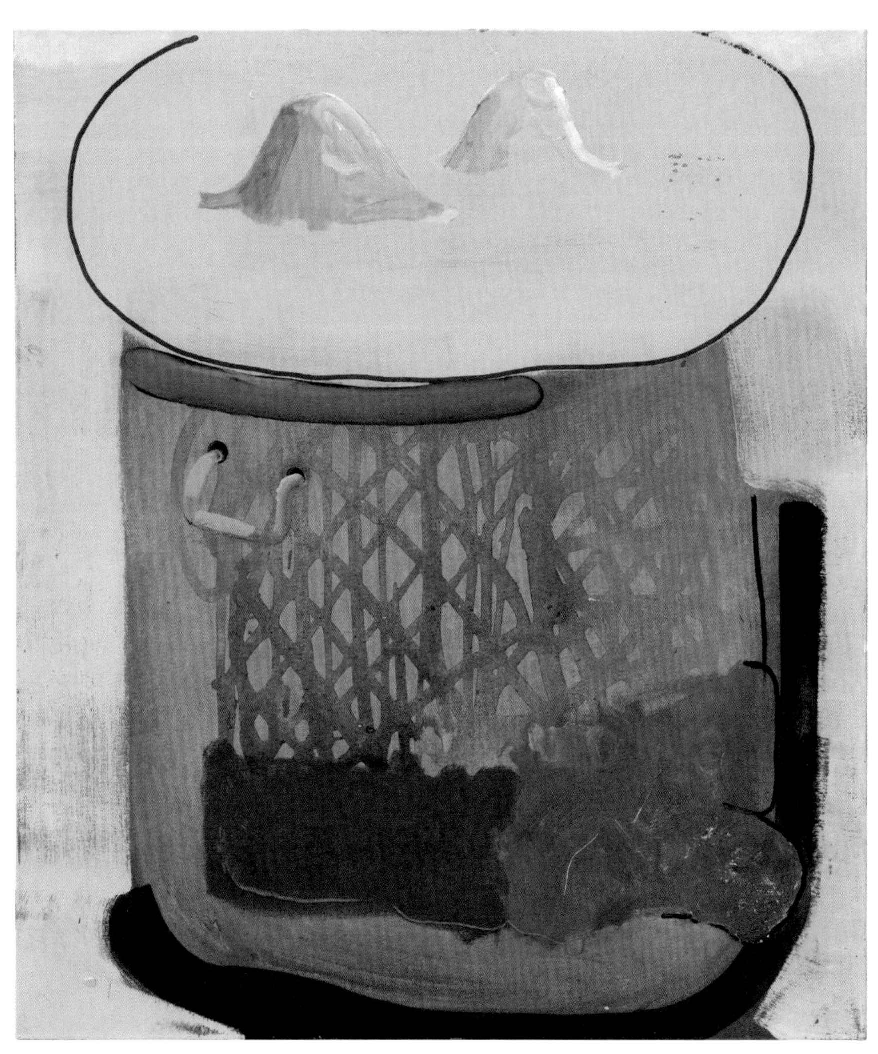

UNTITLED [2016]
Oil, lacquer on canvas | 125 × 105 cm

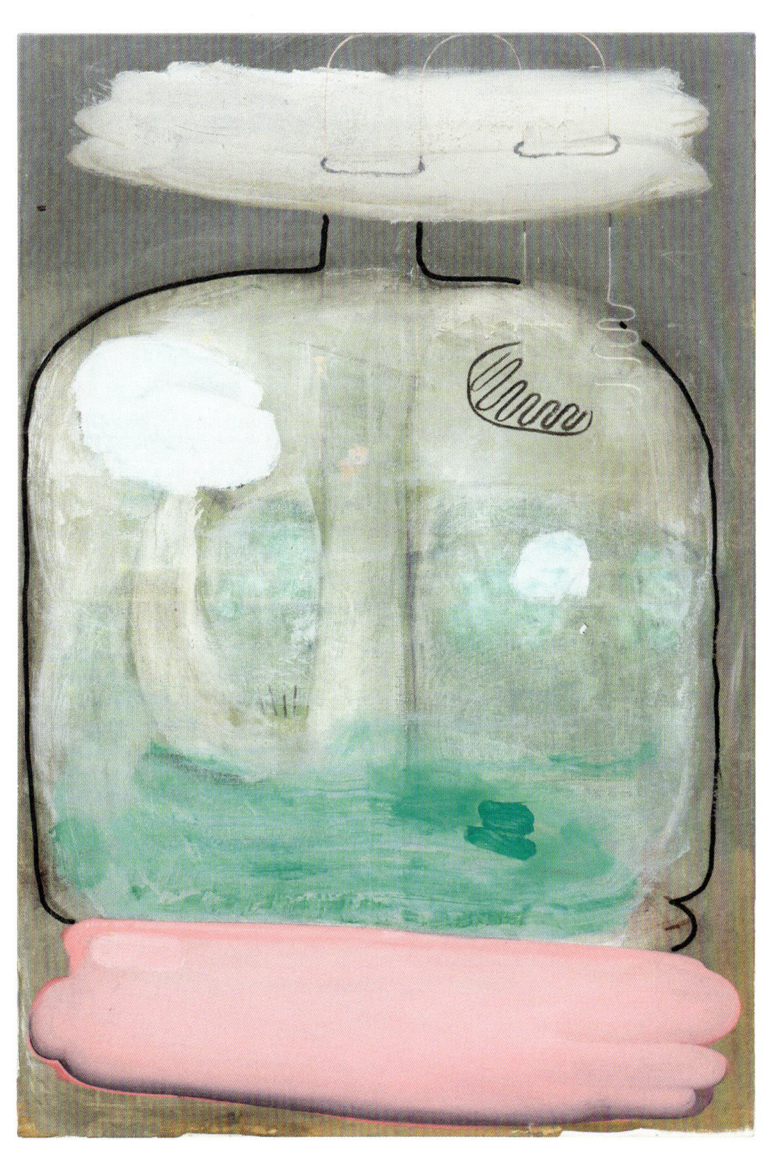

UNTITLED [2016]
Oil, lacquer, charcoal on canvas | 135 × 90 cm

UNTITLED [2014]
Oil, lacquer on canvas | 280 × 200 cm

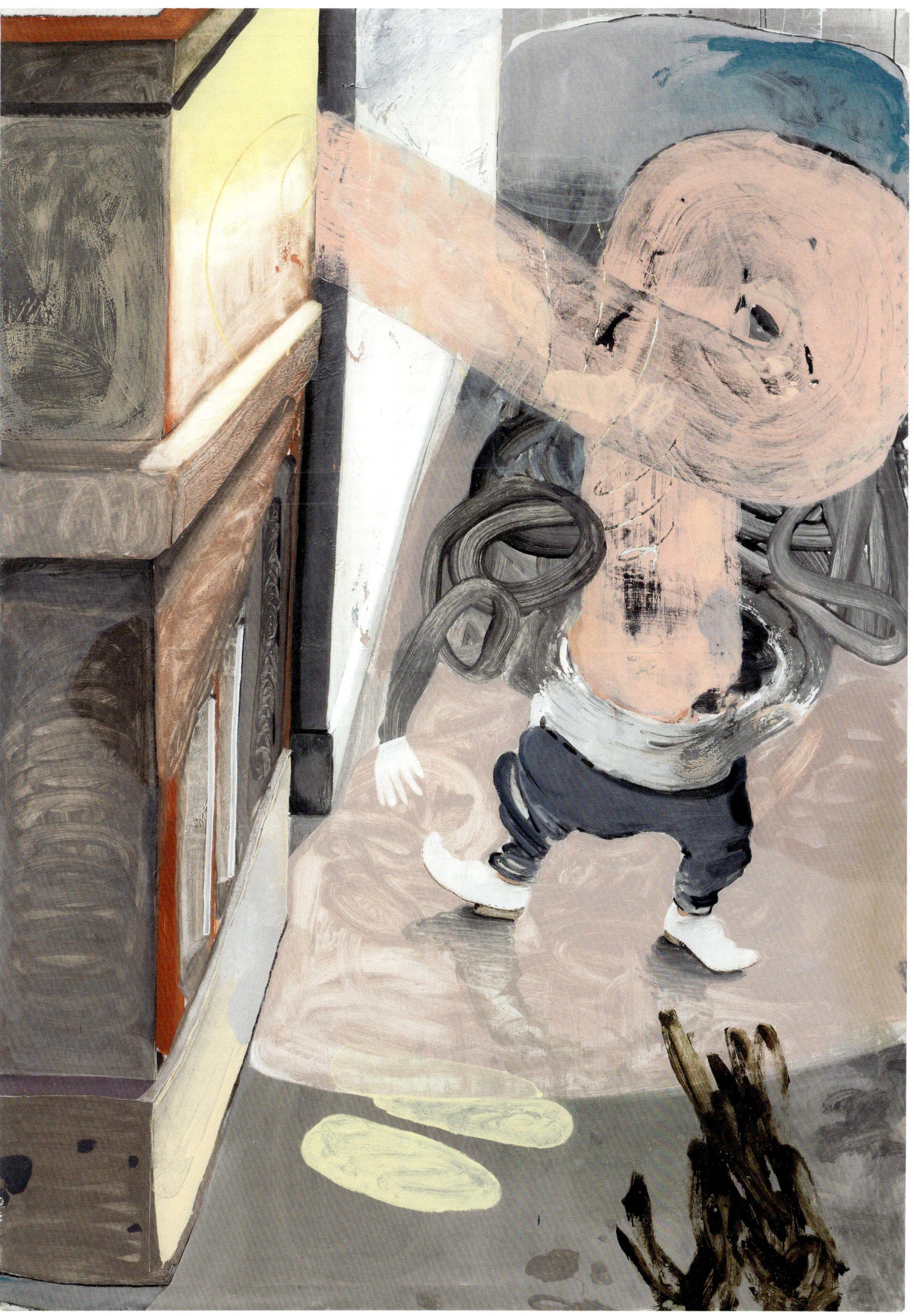

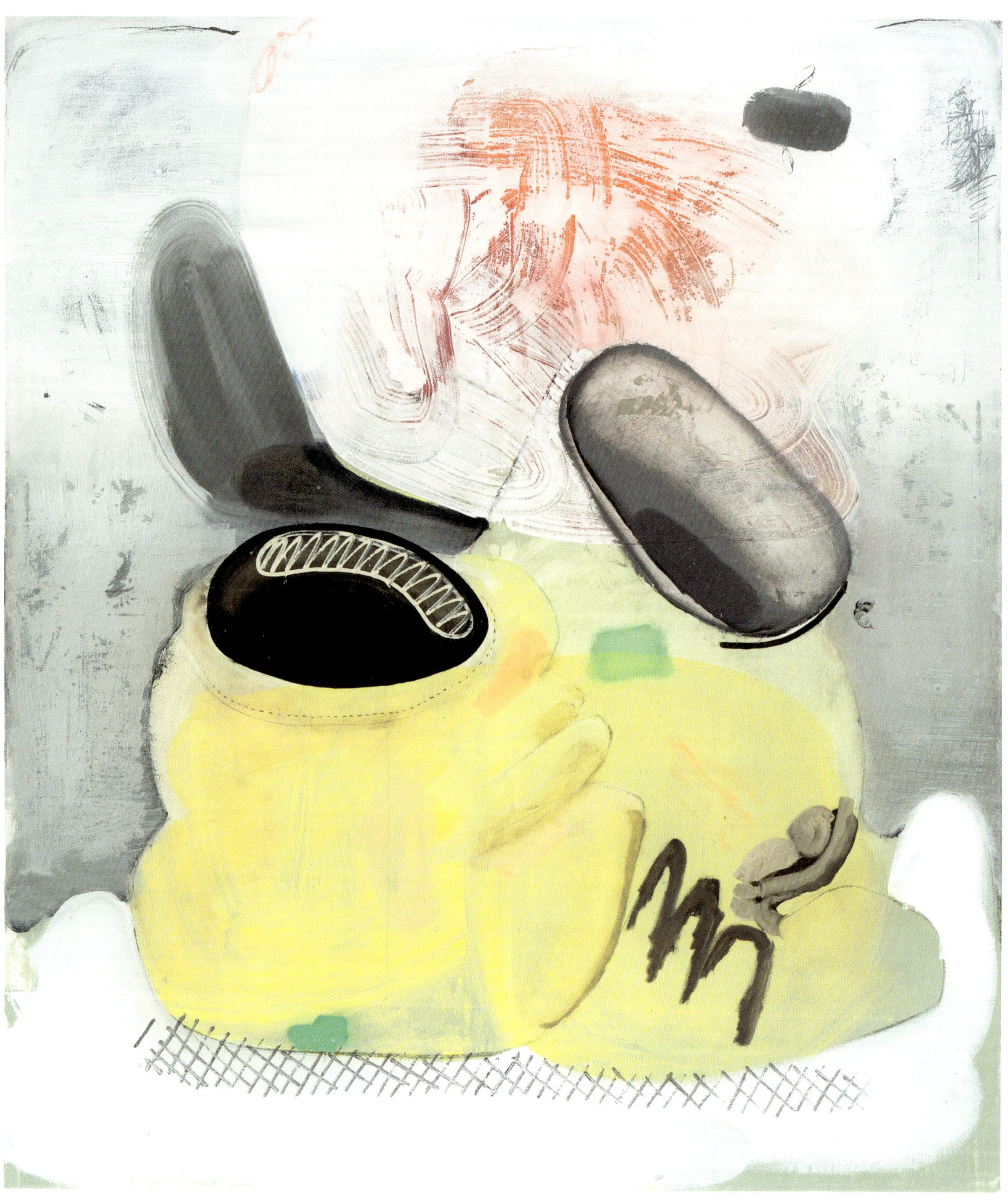

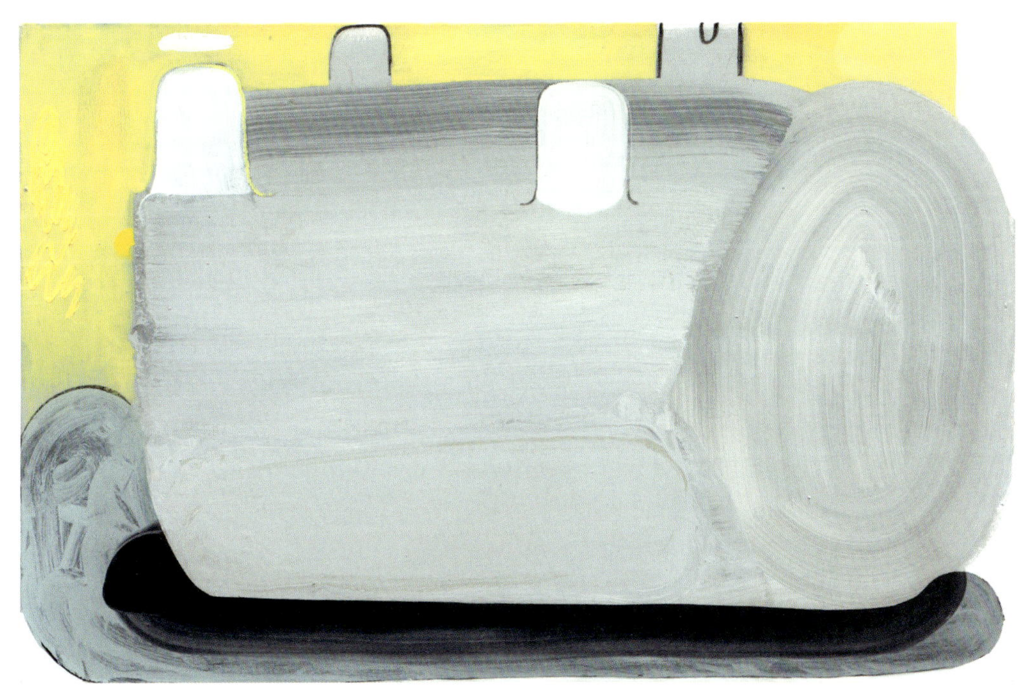

UNTITLED [2015]
Oil, lacquer on canvas | 195 × 165 cm

UNTITLED [2016]
Oil, lacquer, charcoal on canvas | 90 × 135 cm

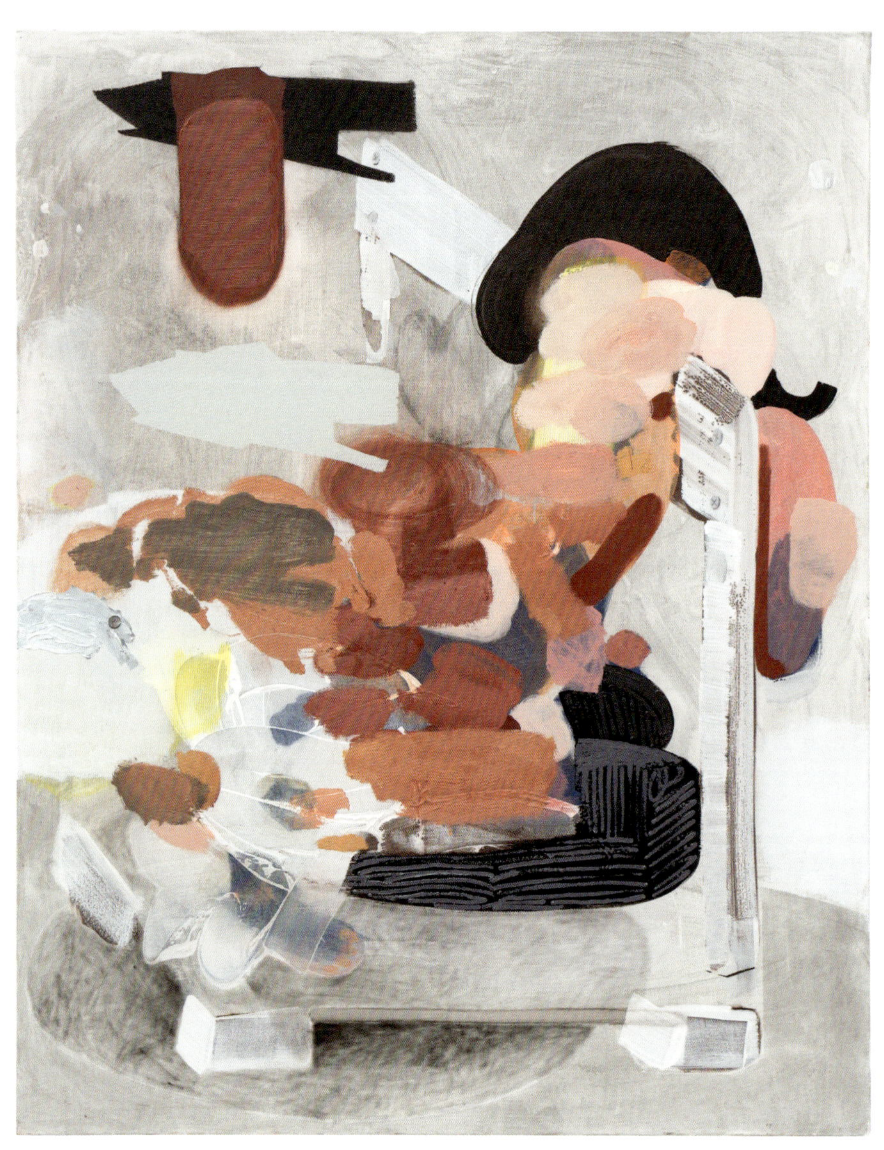

UNTITLED [2014]
Oil, lacquer on canvas | 155 × 120 cm

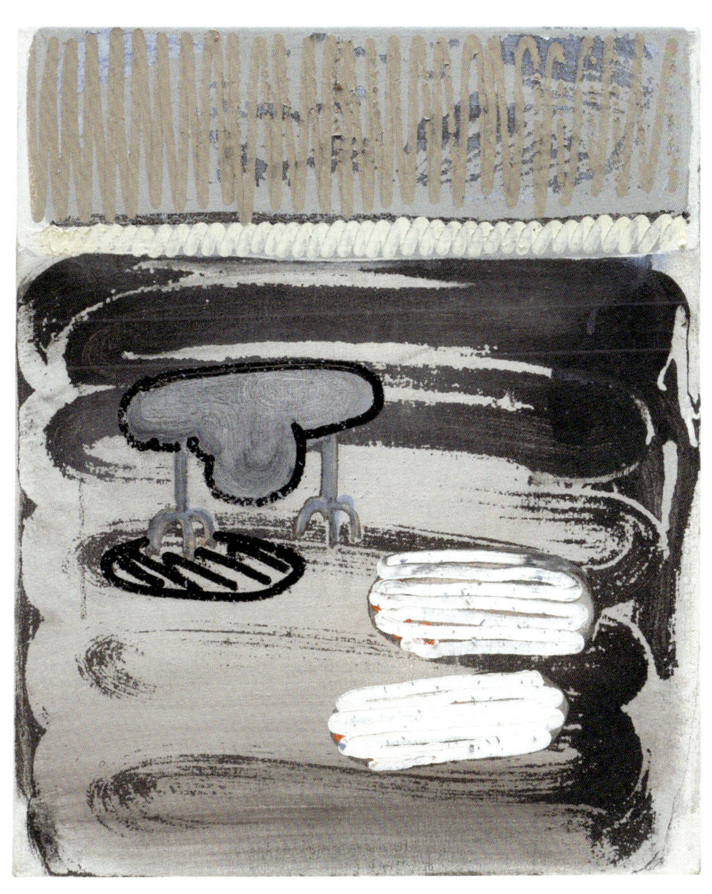

UNTITLED [2016]
Oil, lacquer on canvas | 50 × 40 cm

UNTITLED [2015]
Oil, lacquer on canvas | 295 × 200 cm

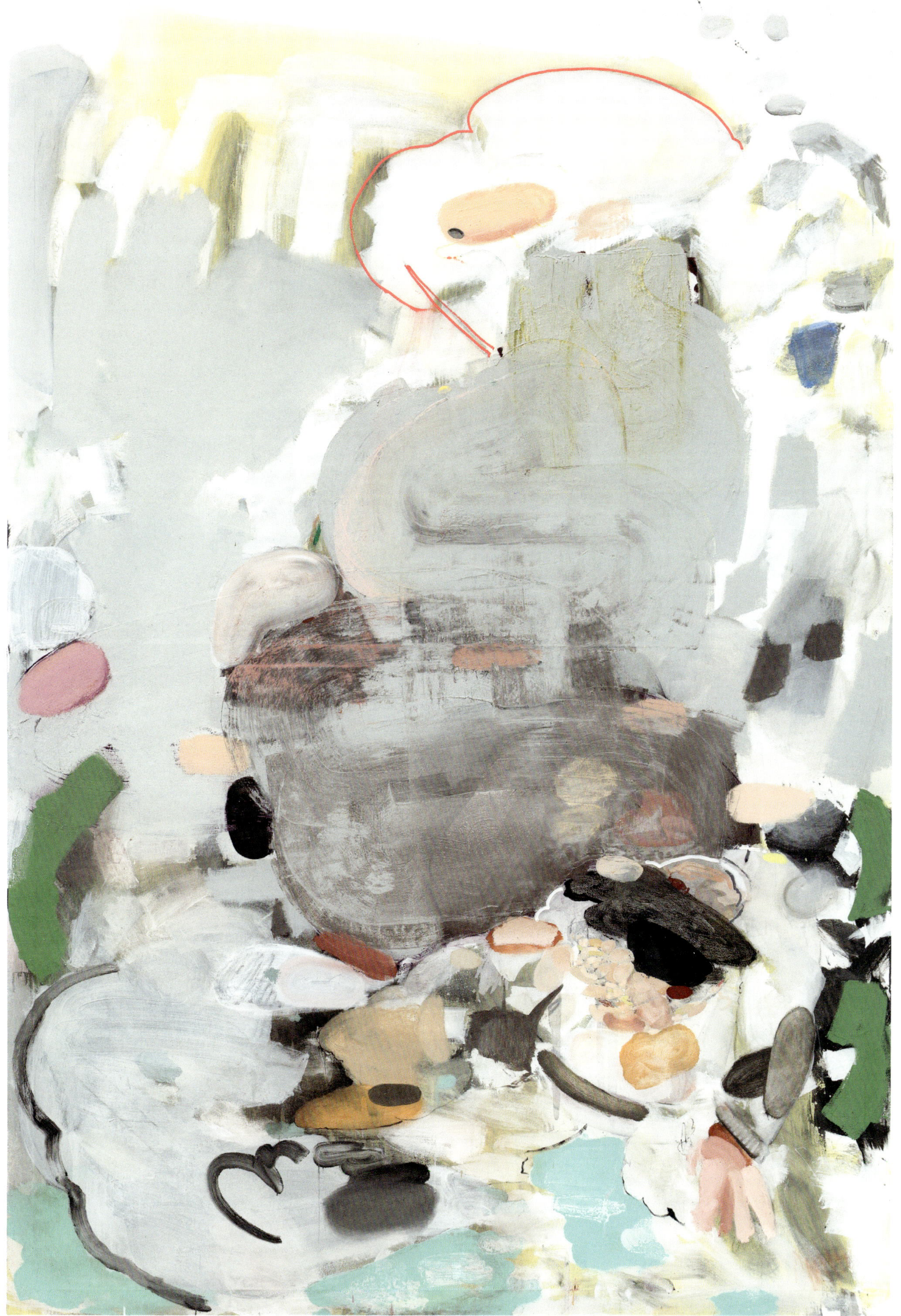

UNTITLED [2014]
Oil, lacquer, charcoal on canvas | 195 × 165 cm

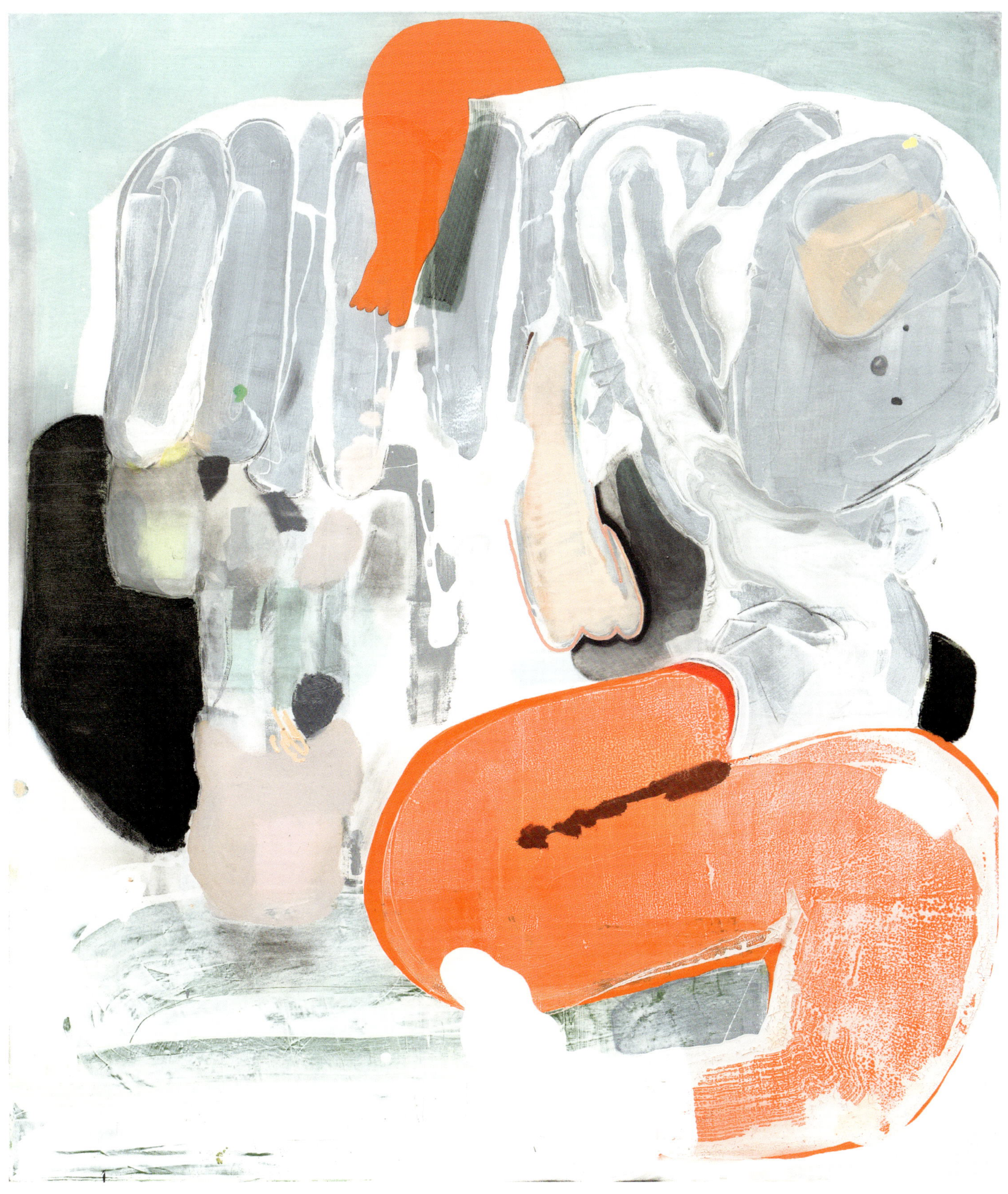

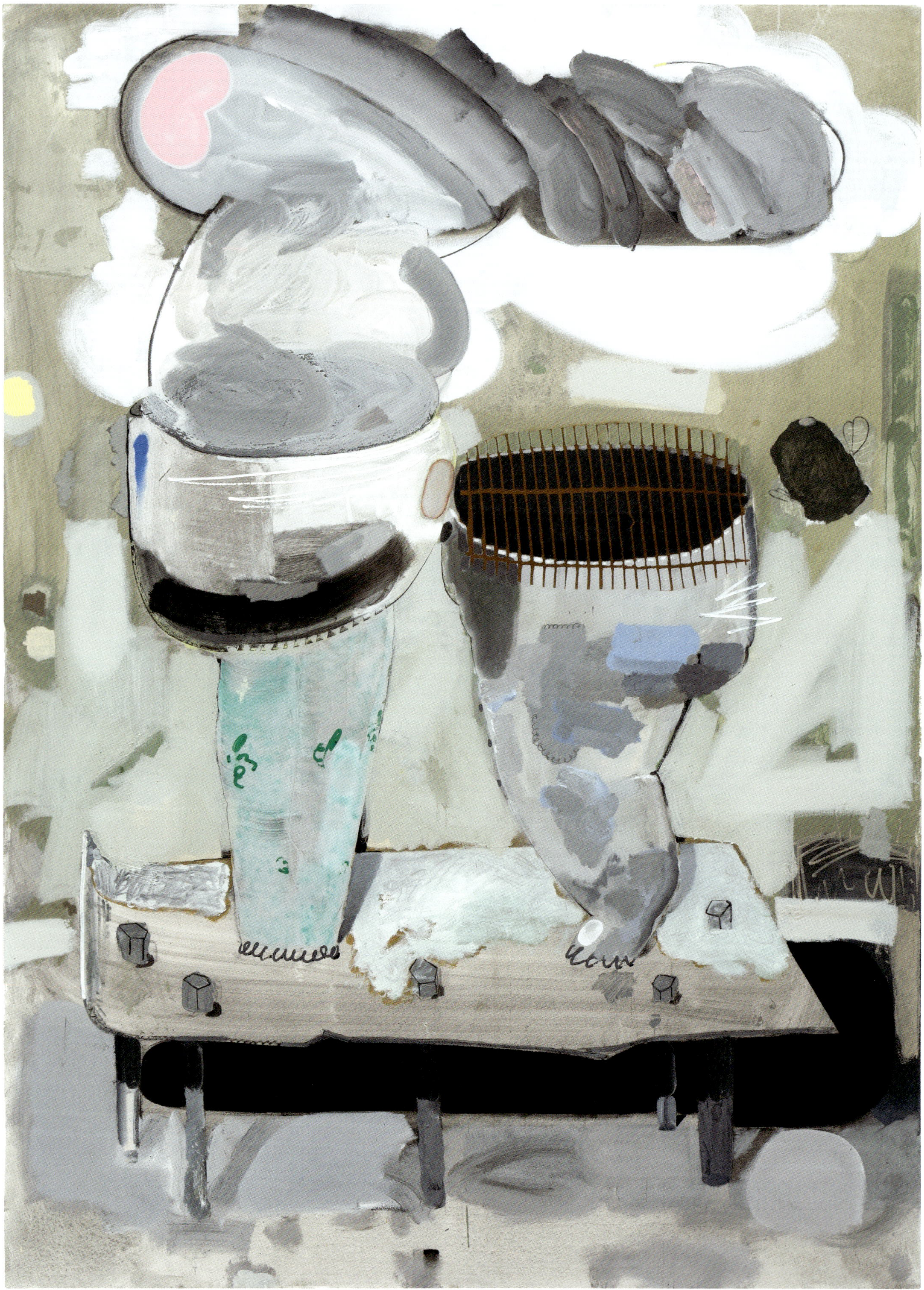

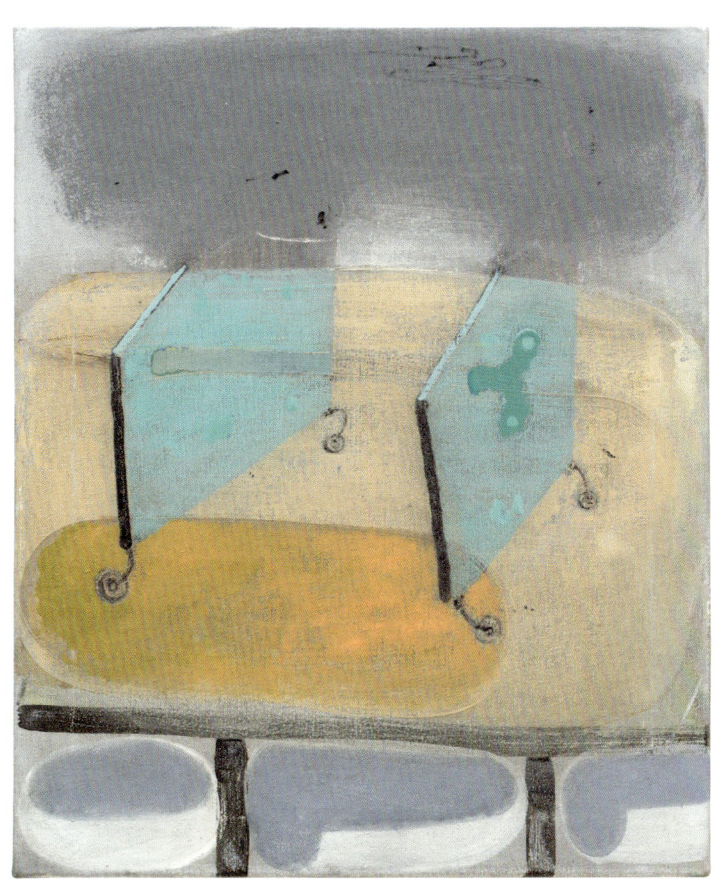

UNTITLED [2016]
Oil, lacquer, charcoal on canvas | 280 × 200 cm

UNTITLED [2016]
Oil, lacquer on canvas | 59 × 48 cm

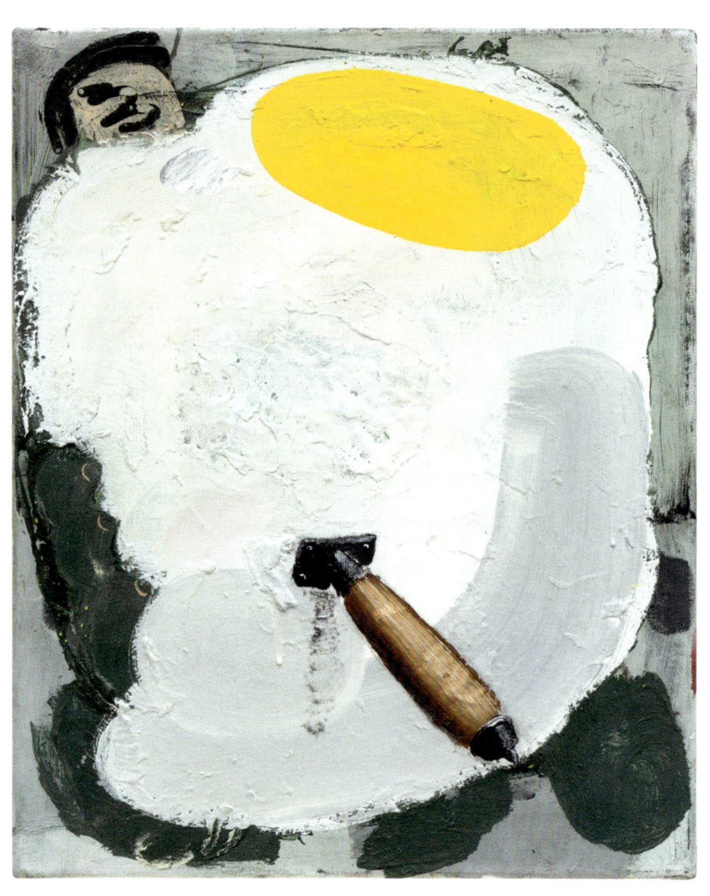

UNTITLED [2016]
Oil, lacquer on canvas | 50 × 40 cm

UNTITLED [2015]
Oil, lacquer, charcoal on canvas | 180 × 160 cm

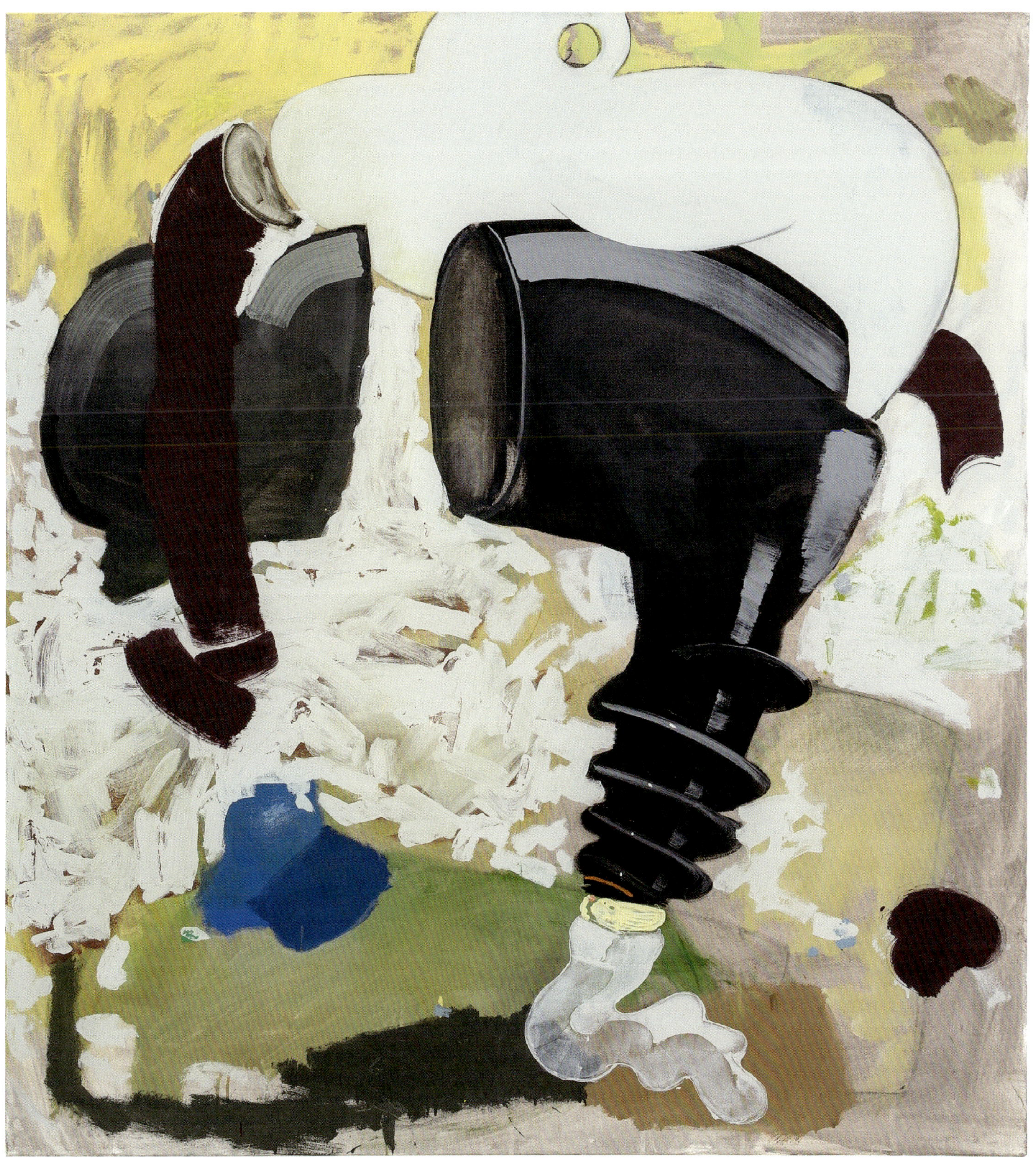

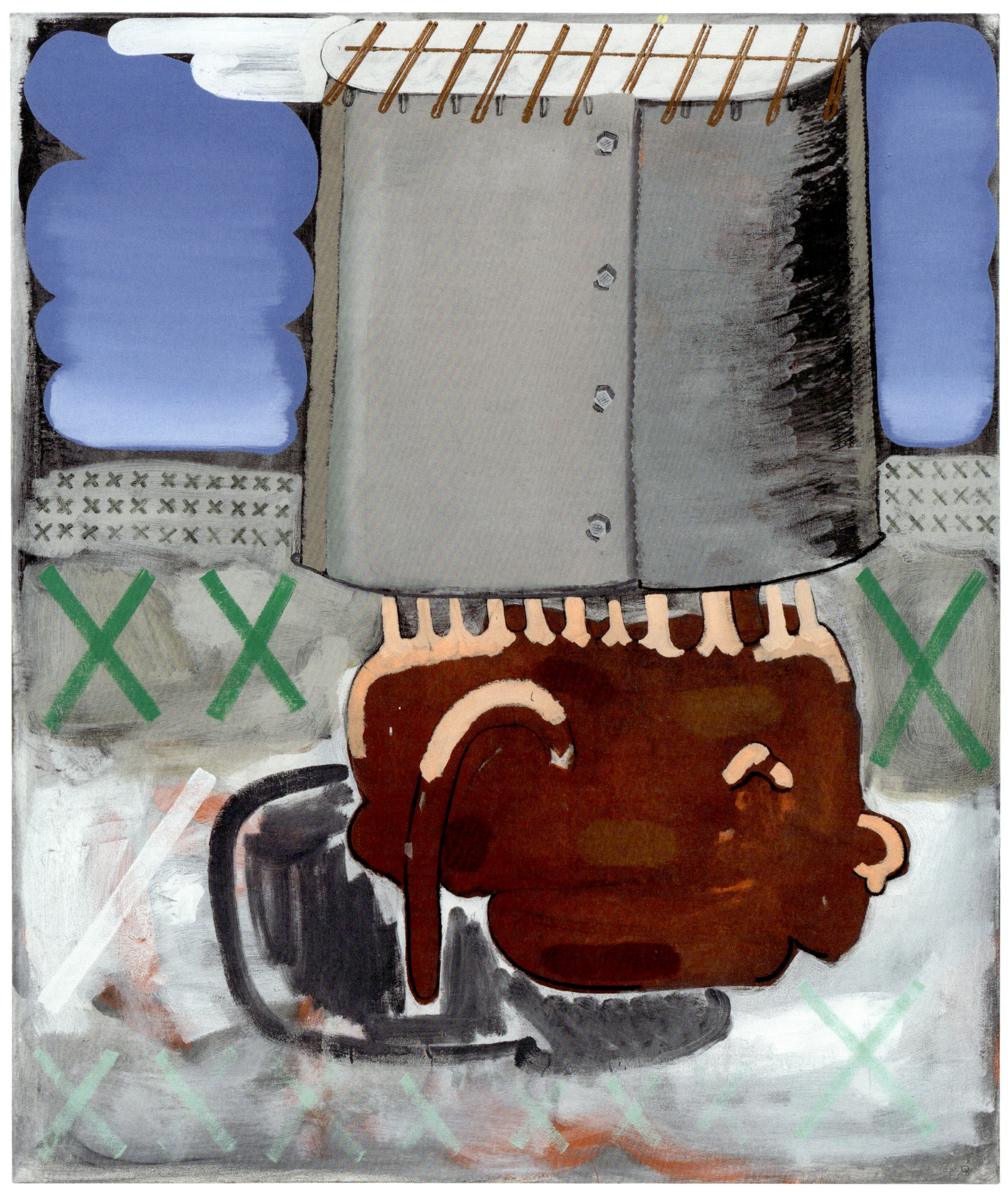

UNTITLED [2016]
Oil, lacquer, charcoal on canvas | 190 × 160 cm

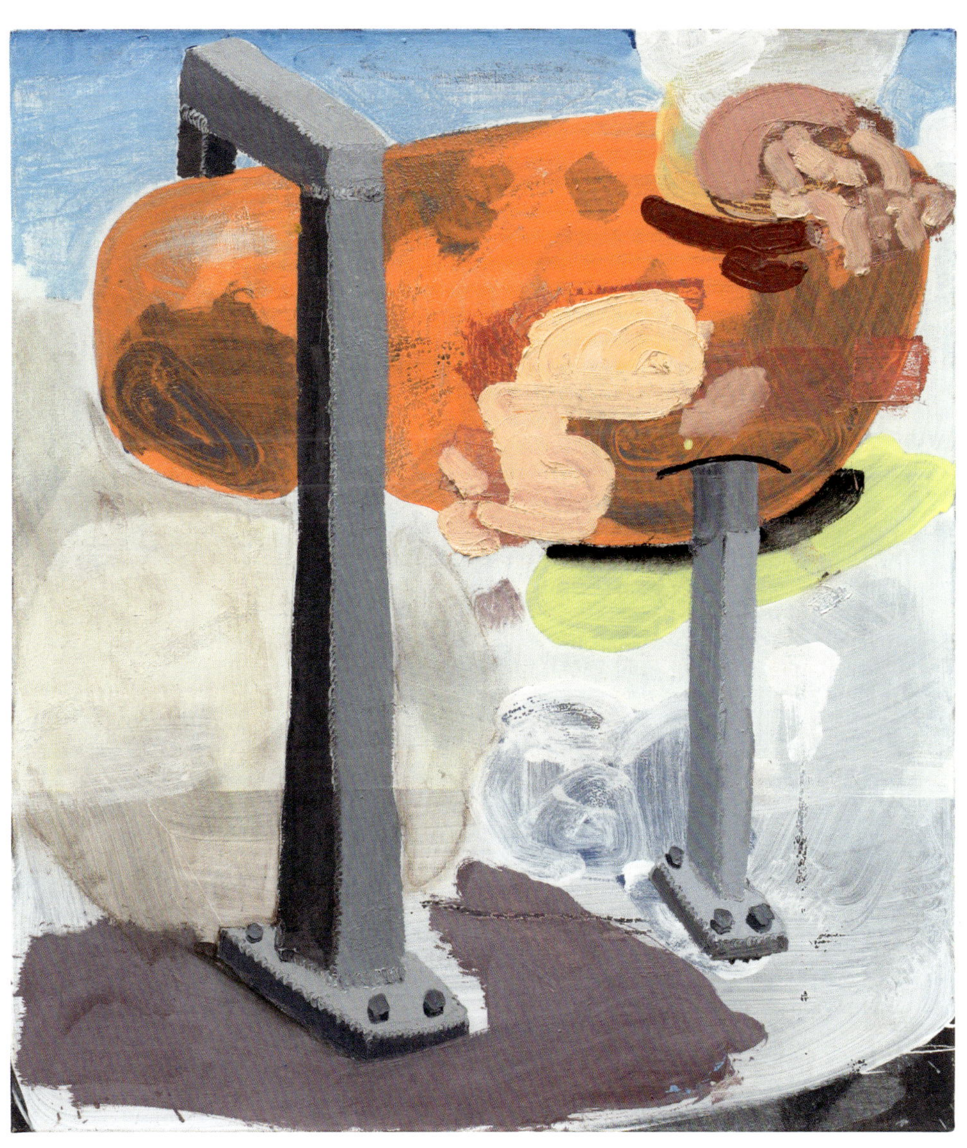

UNTITLED [2015]
Oil, lacquer on canvas | 104 × 89 cm

UNTITLED [2015]

Oil, lacquer on canvas | 199 × 169 cm

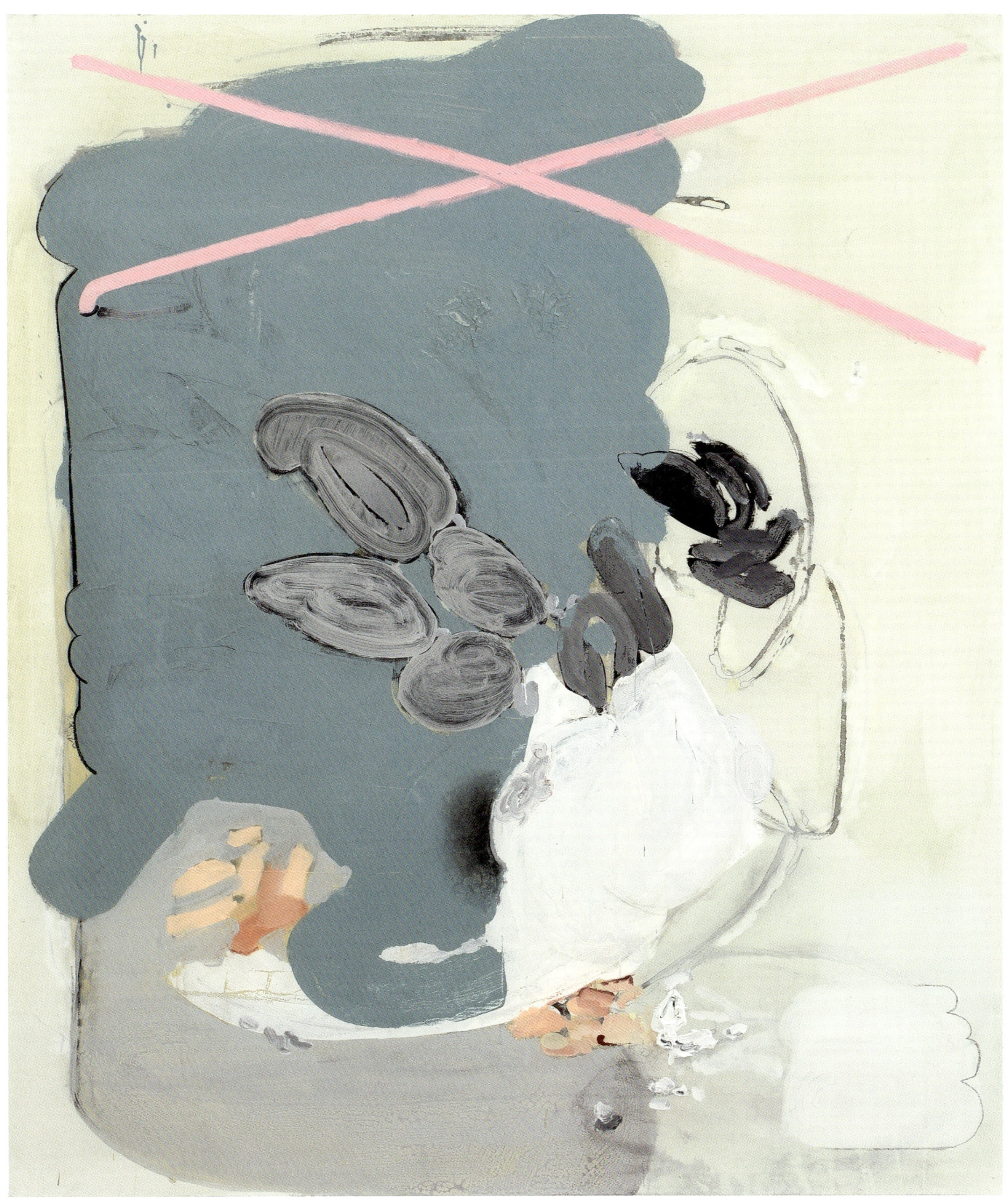

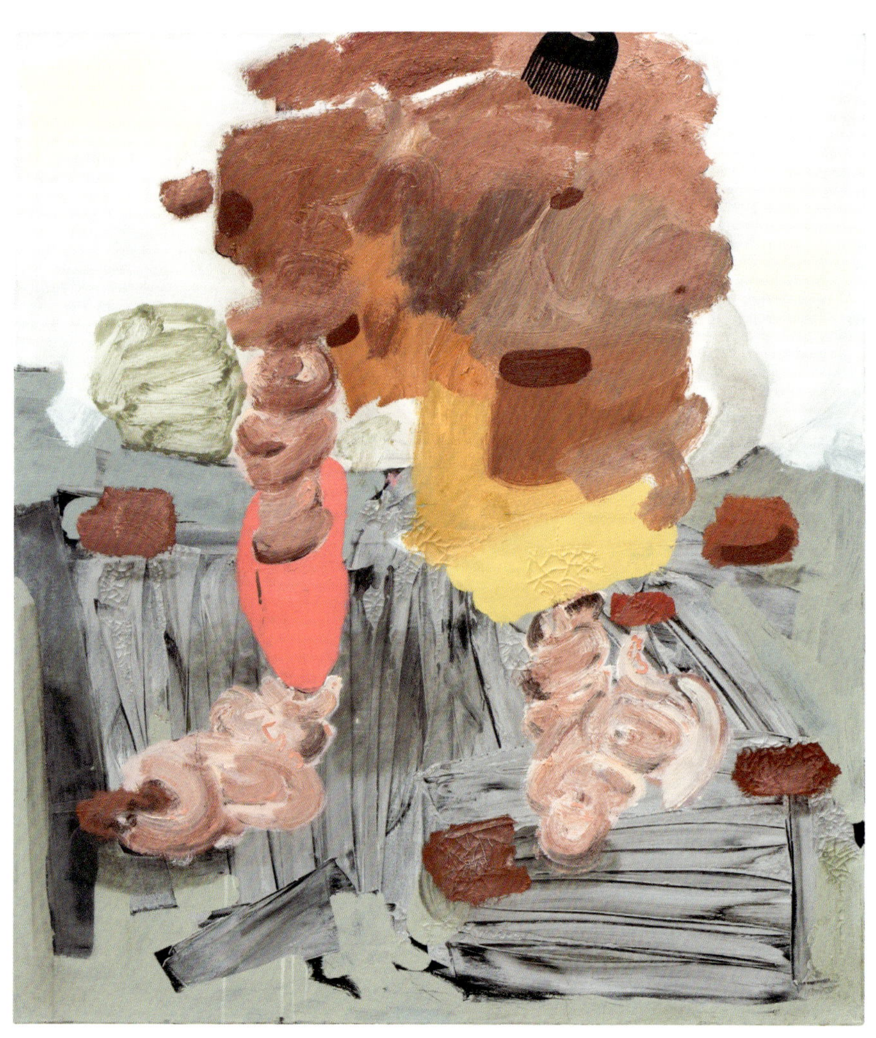

UNTITLED [2015]
Oil, lacquer on canvas | 140 × 120 cm

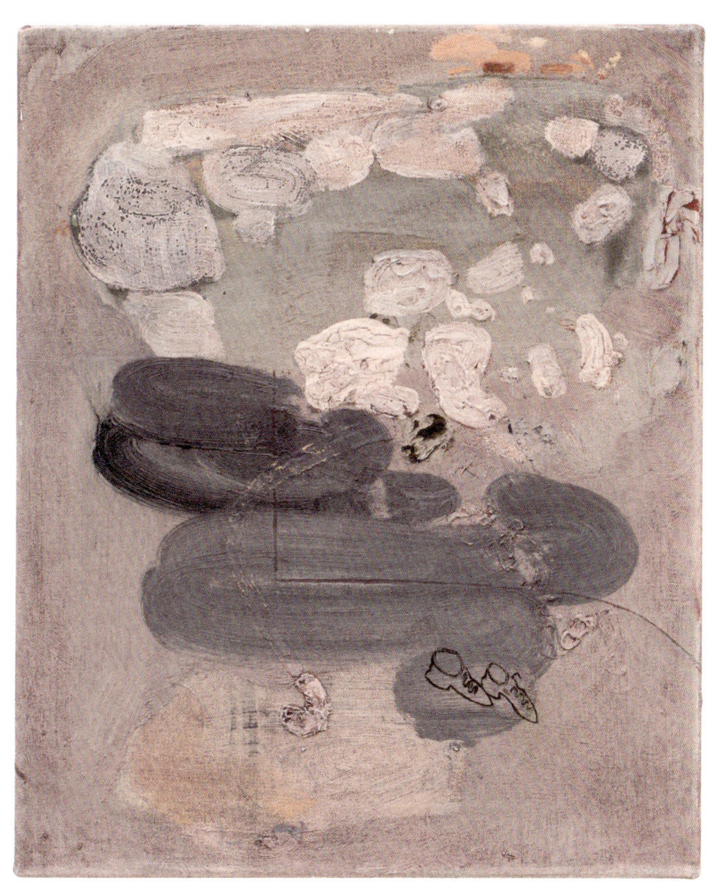

UNTITLED [2014]
Oil, lacquer on canvas | 50 × 40 cm

UNTITLED [2013]

Oil, lacquer on canvas | 285 × 185 cm

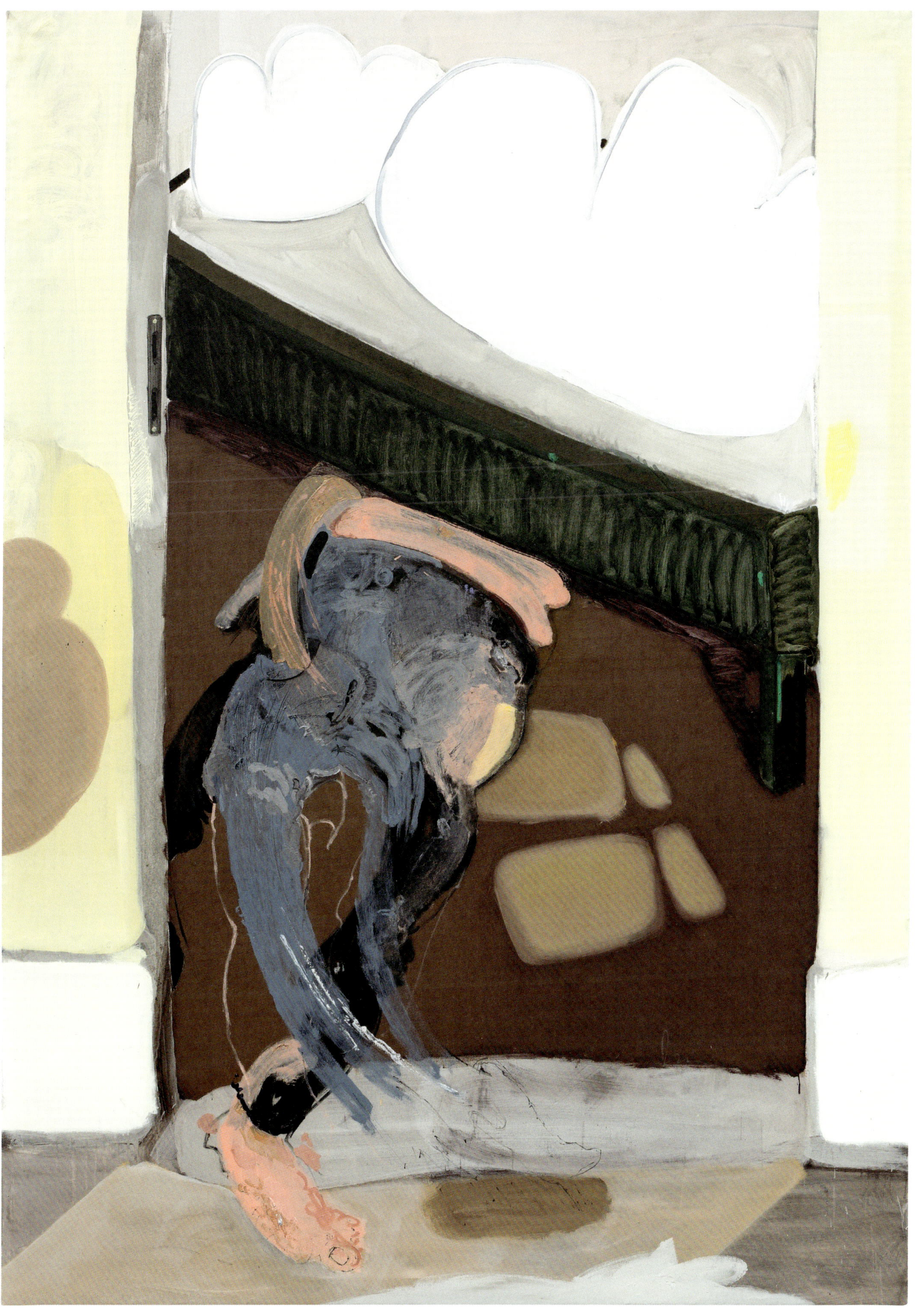

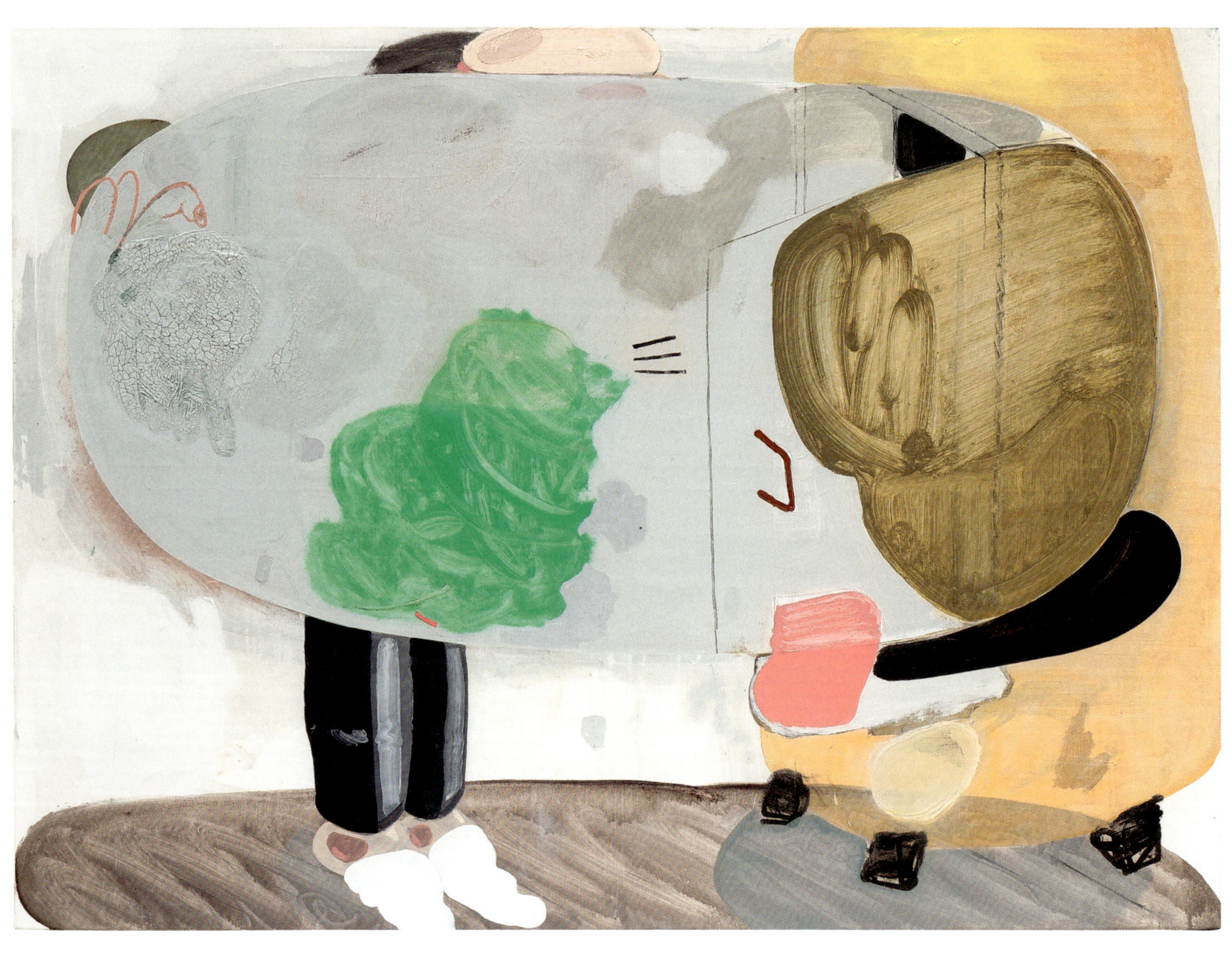

UNTITLED [2014]
Oil, lacquer, charcoal on canvas | 165 × 190 cm

UNTITLED [2016, Detail]
Oil, lacquer, charcoal on canvas | 280 × 200 cm

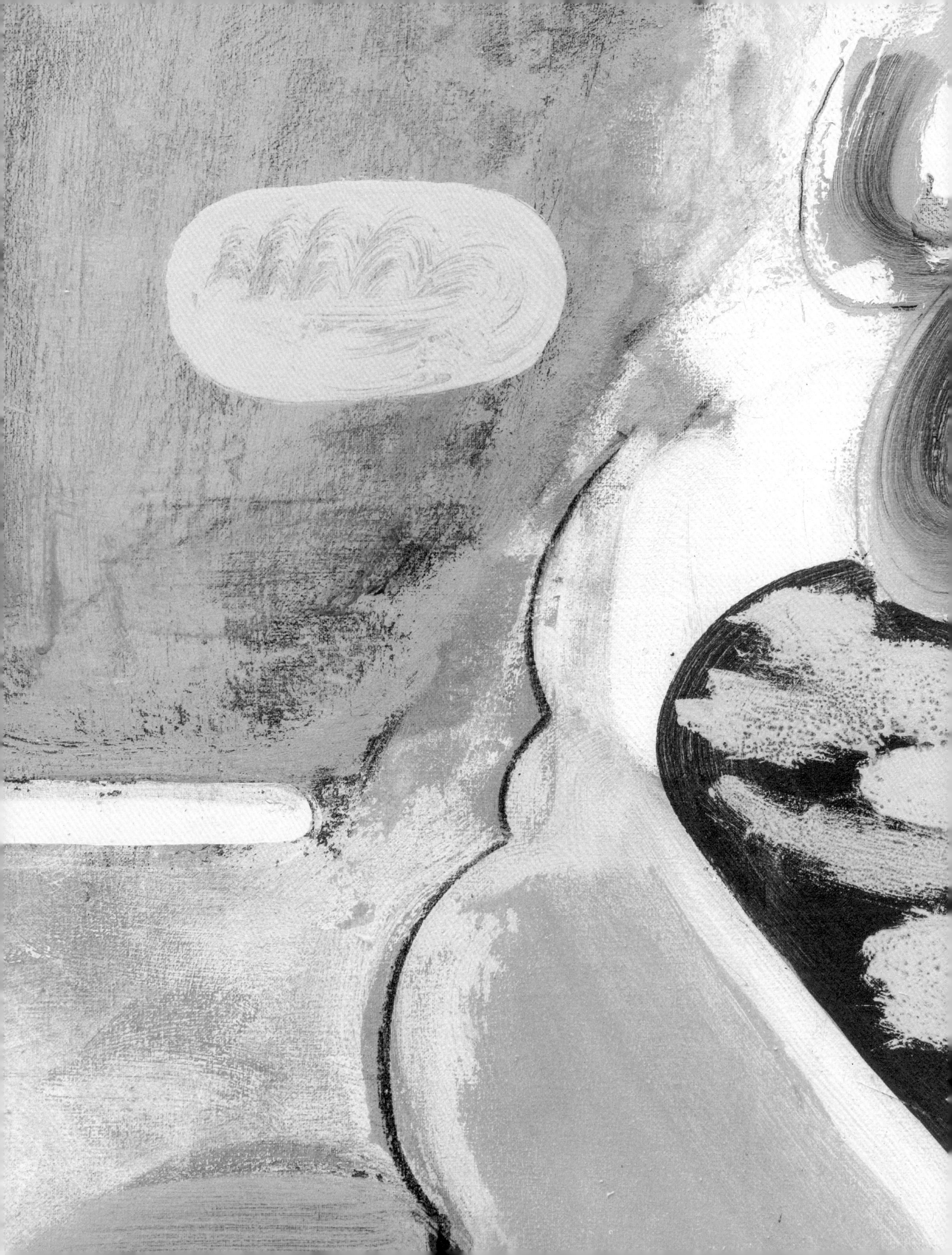

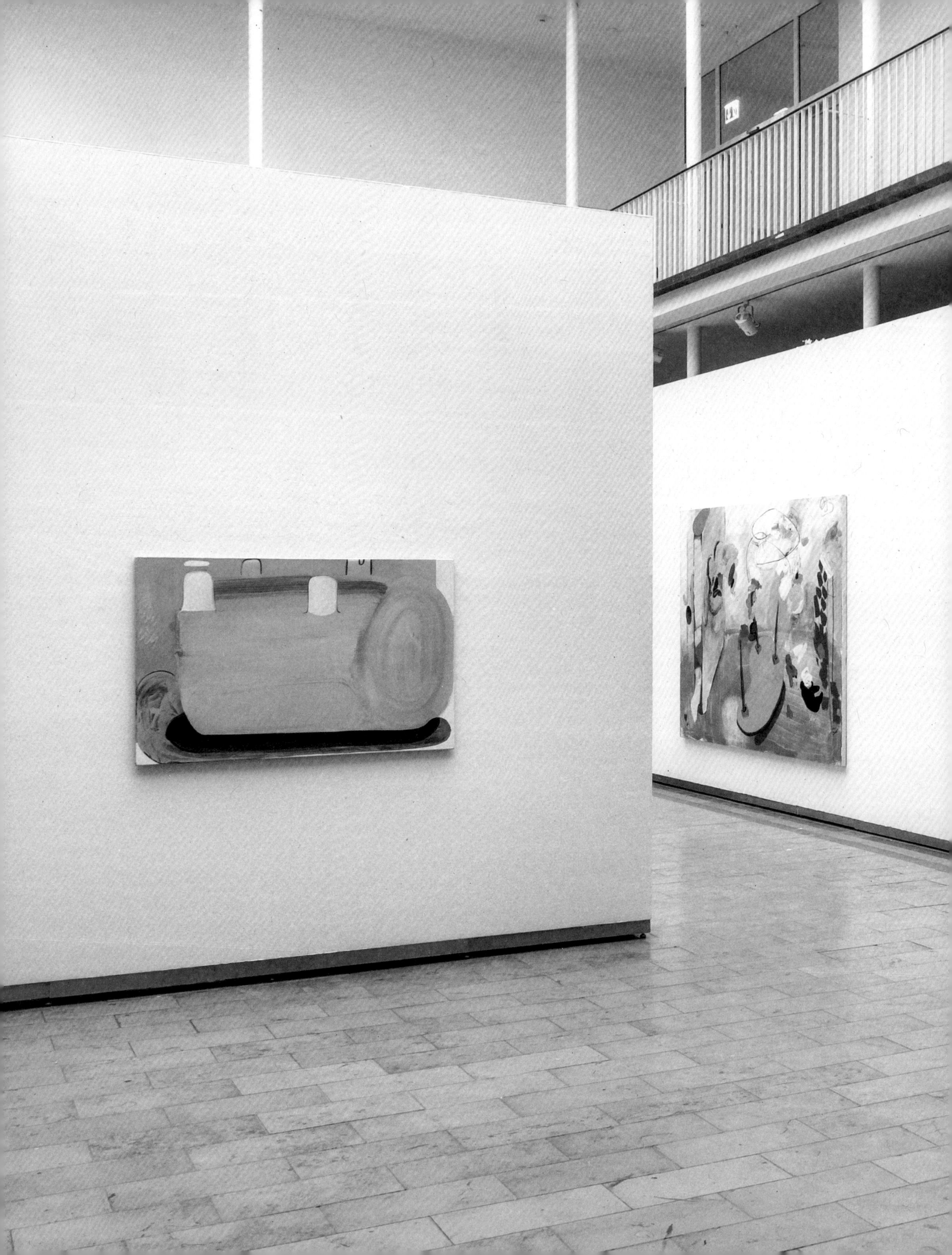

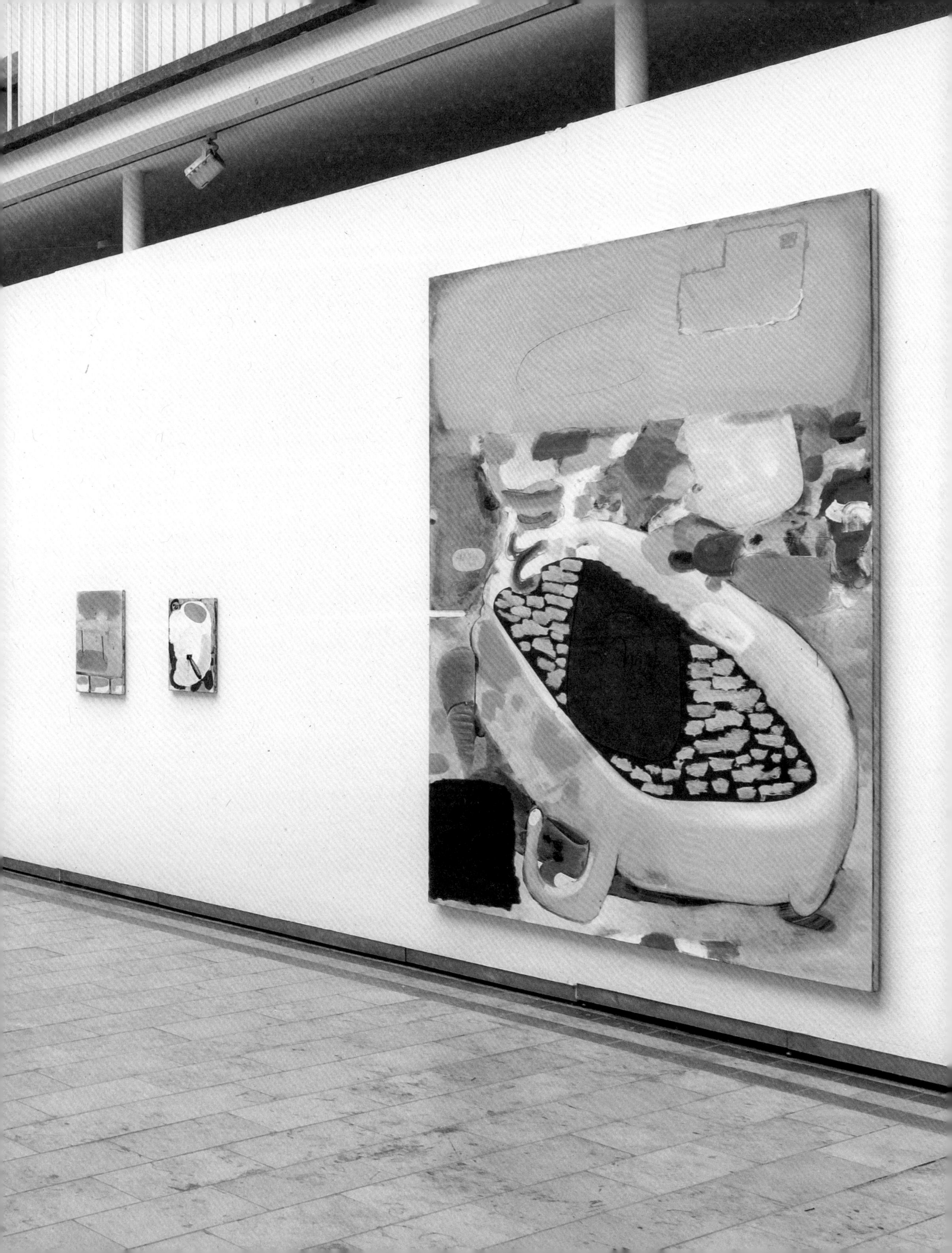

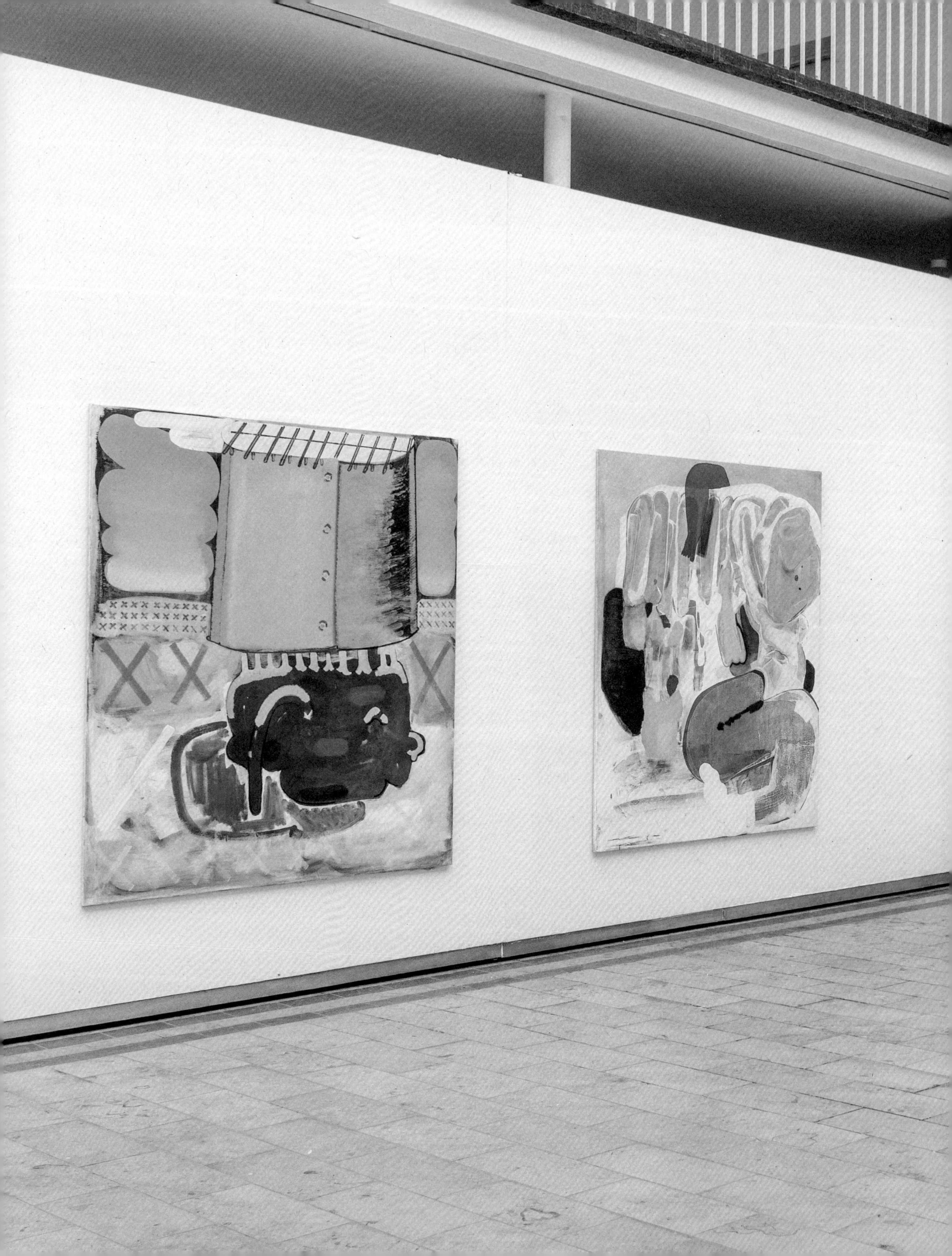

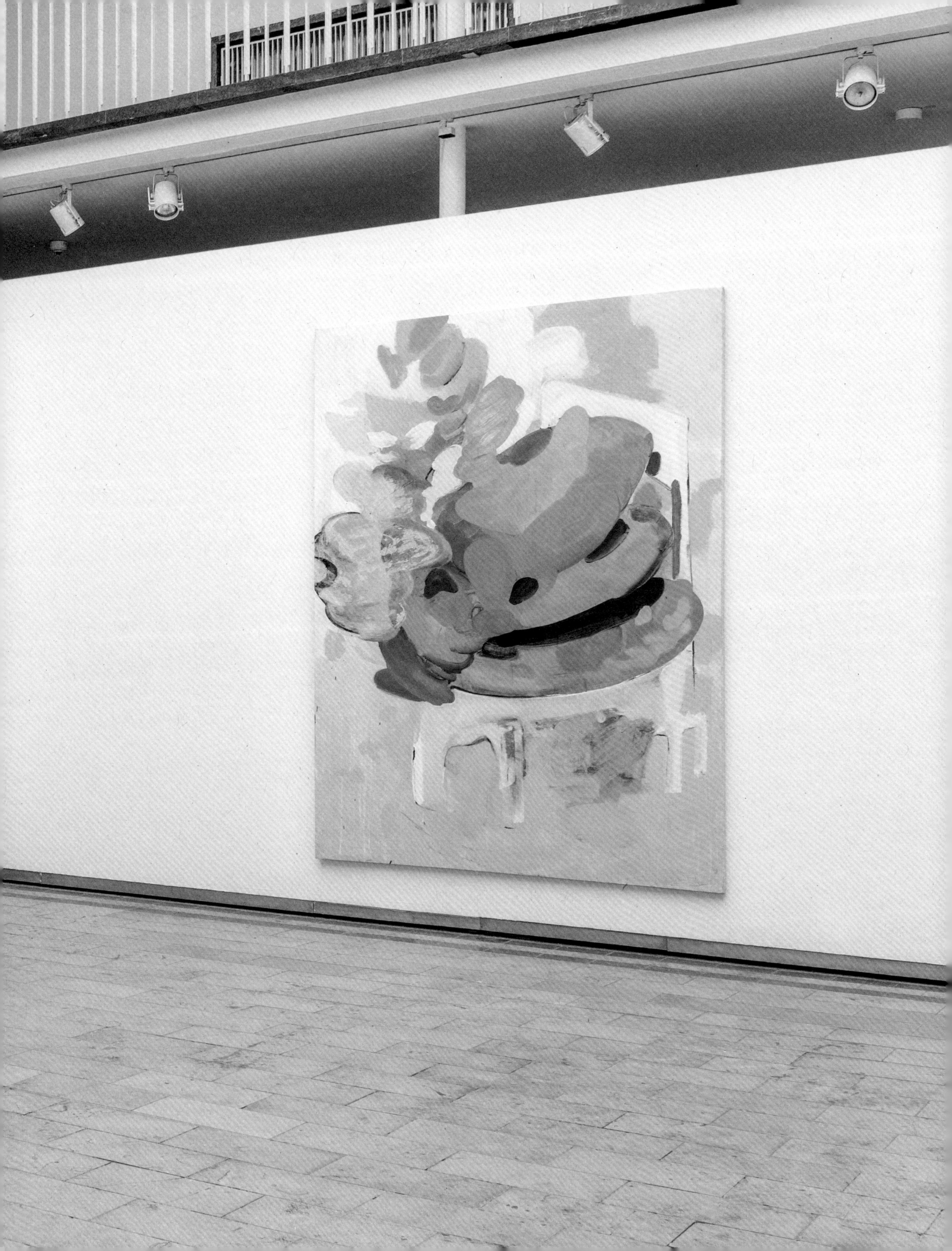

1984	geboren in Schwäbisch Hall, lebt und arbeitet in Karlsruhe
2005 – 10	Staatliche Akademie der Bildenden Künste Karlsruhe bei Prof. Erwin Gross
2008	Akademie der Bildenden Künste Warschau, Erasmus Stipendium
2010 – 12	Aufbaustudium Staatliche Akademie der Bildenden Künste Karlsruhe bei Prof. Erwin Gross

AUSSTELLUNGEN

2016	**OFFENE ATELIERS**, Nordbecken, Karlsruhe
2015	**STOKED**, Galerie WAGNER+PARTNER, Berlin (solo)
	D´ACCORD, Kunst im öffentlichen Raum, Karlsruhe
	THERE ARE GOOD CHANCES TO GET ALONG, Arfmann und Berger, Karlsruhe
	PUMPE, Kunstverein Paderborn (solo mit Xuan Wang)
	MYSTERY BOX, Kunstverein Hohenlohe, Künzelsau (solo)
2014	**BESCHISSEN, VERGESSEN, VERGOLDET**, Nachtspeicher23, Hamburg (solo mit Xuan Wang)
2013	**LOBBY**, Offspace Projekt in Karlsruhe (solo)
2012	**REGIONALE 13**, Kunsthalle Liestal (CH)
2011	**REGIONALE 12**, Kunstraum M54, Basel (CH)
	UTOPIA PARKWAYS, Stuttgart (mit Kyra Beck und Joel Roters)
2010	**NECKARSTEINACH**, Offspace Projekt in Karlsruhe
2007	**KLASSENAUSSTELLUNG**, Kunstverein Schwäbisch Hall

PREISE / STIPENDIEN

2015	Kulturstipendium der Stadt Karlsruhe
2014	Kunststiftung Baden-Württemberg
2012	Graduierten-Stipendium des Landes Baden-Württemberg
2010	Heinrich-Hertz-Preis
2008	Kulturpreis der Stadt Karlsruhe

BASTIAN BÖRSIG [2016]

Ausstellungsansichten / Exhibition views Staatliche Akademie der Bildenden Künste Karlsruhe

1984 born in Schwäbisch Hall, lives and works in Karlsruhe
2005–10 State Academy of Fine Arts Karlsruhe with Prof. Erwin Gross
2008 Academy of Fine Arts Warsaw, Erasmus Scholarship
2010–12 Postgraduate studies at the State Academy of Fine Arts Karlsruhe with Prof. Erwin Gross

EXHIBITIONS

2016 **OPEN STUDIOS**, Nordbecken, Karlsruhe
2015 **STOKED**, Galerie WAGNER+PARTNER, Berlin (solo)
D´ACCORD, art in public places, Karlsruhe
THERE ARE GOOD CHANCES TO GET ALONG, Arfmann and Berger, Karlsruhe
PUMPE, Kunstverein Paderborn (solo with Xuan Wang)
MYSTERY BOX, Kunstverein Hohenlohe, Künzelsau (solo)
2014 **BESCHISSEN, VERGESSEN, VERGOLDET**, Nachtspeicher23, Hamburg (solo with Xuan Wang)
2013 **LOBBY**, offspace project in Karlsruhe (solo)
2012 **REGIONALE 13**, Kunsthalle Liestal (CH)
2011 **REGIONALE 12**, Kunstraum M54, Basel (CH)
UTOPIA PARKWAYS, Stuttgart (with Kyra Beck and Joel Roters)
2010 **NECKARSTEINACH**, offspace project in Karlsruhe
2007 **CLASS EXHIBITION,** Kunstverein Schwäbisch Hall

GRANTS / AWARDS

2015 Cultural Fellowship of Karlsruhe
2014 Art Foundation of Baden-Württemberg
2012 Postgraduate Scholarship of the State of Baden-Württemberg
2010 Heinrich Hertz Award
2008 Culture Award Karlsruhe

IMPRESSUM / COLOPHON

Dieser Katalog erscheint anlässlich der Ausstellung
BASTIAN BÖRSIG
Staatliche Akademie der Bildenden Künste Karlsruhe,
20.–29. April 2016

This catalogue is published on the occasion of the exhibition
BASTIAN BÖRSIG
State Academy of Fine Arts Karlsruhe
April 20 – April 29, 2016

HERAUSGEBER / EDITORS
Cai Wagner und / and Susanne Massmann
für / for Galerie Wagner Massmann

GESTALTUNG / DESIGN
Christian Ertel

TEXTE / TEXTS
Isabella Gerstner, Marc Wellmann

ÜBERSETZUNGEN / TRANSLATIONS
Gerrit Jackson

LEKTORAT / COPY EDITING
DISTANZ, Frederik Kugler

FOTONACHWEIS / PHOTO CREDITS
Bastian Börsig [S./pp. 5–56]
Christian Ertel [S./pp. 2; 57–61]

PRODUKTION / PRODUCTION MANAGEMENT
Antonio Spano, Nino Druck

GESAMTHERSTELLUNG / PRODUCTION
Nino Druck GmbH, Neustadt / WStr.

VERTRIEB / DISTRIBUTION
Gestalten, Berlin
www.gestalten.com
sales@gestalten.com

ISBN 978-3-95476-144-9

Printed in Germany

ERSCHIENEN IM / PUBLISHED BY
DISTANZ Verlag | www.distanz.de

Ausstellung und Katalog wurden gefördert durch / Exhibition and catalogue were supported by

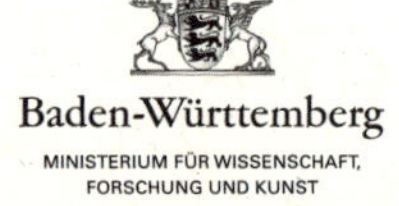